ALL YOU HAVE TO DO IS ASK

ALL YOU HAVE TO DO IS ASK

HOW TO MASTER THE MOST IMPORTANT SKILL FOR SUCCESS

WAYNE BAKER

CURRENCY

NEW YORK

Published in the United States by Currency, an imprint of Random House, a division of Penguin Random House LLC, New York.

CURRENCY and its colophon are trademarks of Penguin Random House LLC.

LIBRARY OF CONGRESS CATALOGING-IN-PUBLICATION DATA
Names: Baker, Wayne E., author.
Title: All you have to do is ask: how to master the most important skill for success / Wayne Baker.
Description: 1. Edition. | New York: Currency, [2020] | Includes bibliographical references and index.
Identifiers: LCCN 2019019501 | ISBN 9781984825926 | ISBN 9781984825933 (ebook)
Subjects: LCSH: Communication in organizations. | Interpersonal relations. | Helping behavior. | Teams in the workplace.
Classification: LCC HD30.3 .B365 2020 | DDC 650.101/4—dc23
LC record available at https://lccn.loc.gov/2019019501

Printed in the United States of America on acid-free paper

currencybooks.com

2 4 6 8 9 7 5 3 1

First Edition

Book design by Jo Anne Metsch

With love to my dear wife,

Cheryl,

and our fabulous son,

Harrison

CONTENTS

———

THE

POWER

OF

"THE ASK"

CHAPTER 1

JUST ASK AND
MIRACLES HAPPEN

Jessica was overwhelmed and didn't know what to do. She is a generous person by nature who had volunteered, as she often does, to help a stressed-out colleague. This time, it was a recent hire at the IT firm where they both worked who was inexperienced with the company's customer relationship management (CRM) system and had fallen behind. Jessica knew the system inside out, so she offered to take over a data-entry task on her colleague's behalf. But what started as a simple favor for a colleague in distress soon grew into a colossal headache for Jessica.[1]

"The additional workload didn't seem overwhelming when I agreed to help," Jessica told me, "but I quickly realized how time-consuming it was." She began coming into the office early, staying late, and working through lunch to keep up with her existing job duties. She became resentful of the rest of her team for going out for lunch, or leaving work at 5:00 P.M. "I was even resentful when people stopped by my office to catch up!" she said. "A fifteen-minute conversation with a coworker meant fifteen minutes I wouldn't be able to spend with my family that evening."

Jessica needed some help of her own. But she never asked for it. "I assumed that my other team members had full plates also, so I continued to labor through the workload," she explained. "I didn't know how important it was for me to raise my hand and ask for help. I assumed that it was the responsibility of my manager or coworkers to notice how much extra work I was doing and offer to help shoulder the load."

As Jessica's desperation grew, she saw only one solution: quit. And that's what she did. Looking back on her situation, she realized that the problem was never her job or her employer, it was her own failure to ask for the help she needed to get her work done. "I will never make that mistake again!" she said.

Like Jessica, so many of us are reluctant to ask for help when we are overwhelmed. When I ask audiences what it takes for them to ask for help, most people tell me they only speak up once they reach their wit's end.[2] "I ask for help only when I can't figure it out for myself and I'm totally desperate," they say.

If that statement describes you too, you aren't alone. And yet, giving voice to our needs and requests has so many benefits. It makes us more effective at our jobs. It leads us to new job opportunities—or new talent for job openings. It helps us better adjust to new circumstances. It enhances learning and boosts creativity. It elevates team performance and improves operational efficiency. Moreover, studies show that when we do make a request, even total strangers are significantly more likely to grant it than we assume. *Asking for help is often the one simple act standing between us and success.* But, the thought of actually doing so can be terrifying for so many of us.

It's critical to understand that help rarely arrives unasked for. In fact, studies show that as much as 90 percent of the help that is provided in the workplace occurs only *after* requests for help have been made.[3] The explanation is simple. People can't help you if they don't know what you need, and they don't know what you need until you tell them. When we *don't* ask for what we need, the costs are enormous. Research shows that failure to ask for help costs *Fortune 500* companies billions of dollars each year.[4] And the costs in our own lives—at home, work, and everywhere else—are much greater than most of us realize. *Not* asking for help is one of the most self-limiting, self-constraining, even self-destructive decisions we can make. Without the help and assistance of others, we don't receive the resources that we need to get our work done, to solve problems, and to fulfill our missions in the world.

WHEN WE ASK, MIRACLES CAN HAPPEN

Cristina is the youngest of three children. Her parents doted on her from the time she was born. So, as you can imagine, they were devastated when they discovered that something wasn't quite right: her head wasn't developing properly.[5]

It turned out that the joints in her young skull had fused too early. A baby's skull is made of five major bones held together by joints, or cranial sutures, composed of fibrous tissues. If you've felt a soft spot on a baby's head, then you've touched a space between the bones where the sutures intersect. These flexible sutures allow a baby's brain and head to grow. Cristina's cranial sutures closed prematurely, preventing normal development. This rare condition is called "craniosynostosis." Left untreated, it results in a permanently misshapen head and distorted face, which likely means a lifetime of ridicule and social isolation. And the condition carries a high risk of developmental delays, learning problems, blindness, seizures, or even death.

Specialized surgery could correct the shape of Cristina's skull and allow her brain to grow and develop normally. But in Romania, where Cristina's family lives, finding a specialist who could perform this rare and delicate surgery was a long shot. Without a miracle, this little girl's future was in jeopardy.

It so happened that Cristina's aunt, Felicia, who lives in France and works at INSEAD, one of the world's premiere business schools, had volunteered to facilitate an activity called the "Reciprocity Ring" as part of the new-student orientation program. You'll learn more about the Reciprocity Ring in Part II of this book, but for now, think of it as a guided group activity that allows participants to tap the collective knowledge, wisdom, and resources of a large network to obtain things they need. All incoming MBAs at INSEAD participate in the activity.

As part of her training, Felicia participated in two rounds of the Reciprocity Ring. The first round was for personal requests, the second for work-related requests. Initially, Felicia didn't know what to ask for in the first round. But she mustered the courage to ask for the one thing that could reverse her young niece's fate: an experienced pediatric cranial surgeon who knew how to remedy craniosynostosis.

That day, an adjunct professor of Organisational Behaviour at INSEAD named Dr. Thomas Hellwig also was being trained to run a Reciprocity Ring. At the time, Dr. Hellwig worked as a psychotherapist and pediatrician at Necker, a children's hospital in Paris, and when he heard Felicia's heartfelt request, he knew he had to help. So, he responded with an offer to assist, which led to a connection to Dr. Eric Arnaud, a surgeon at Necker and Marcel Sembat (another children's hospital in the area), who was a seasoned specialist in the very procedure Cristina required.

After a flurry of email exchanges and phone calls, Cristina and her parents flew to France, where Cristina had the surgery at Marcel Sembat to correct her condition. It was a success, and today Cristina is thriving. I keep a picture of her on my desk as a testimony and a reminder of the tremendous power of asking for what we need.

I have thousands of stories like Cristina's—perhaps not as dramatic, but just as unlikely. Or I should say *seemingly* unlikely. When we give ourselves permission to ask, we unlock human generosity and miracles happen.

WHY ASK?

A senior engineer at a major auto company was struggling to solve a complex technical problem. He'd been going around in circles on it for months, in fact, and was getting nowhere. Then one day he decided it was time to seek some help. So, he reached out to his network of colleagues, described the problem, and asked if anyone knew an expert he could consult with. Much to his surprise, the first person to respond wasn't one of the senior research scientists, or an engineer in a different unit. Instead, help came from an unlikely source: a 22-year-old administrative assistant who had just been hired by the company. Turned out that her father was one of the world's experts in the very process the engineer was struggling with. What's more, he had recently retired—and his wife was encouraging him to spend more time out of the house. The admin introduced the engineer to her father, and the engineer got the expertise he needed.

This example illustrates a crucial point: you never know what people know—or who they know—until you ask. No one would have thought that a young admin would hold the keys to the solution. If you just ask for what you need, help will come, sometimes from the place you least expect it.

In the workplace, asking for help can mean the difference between success and failure. This isn't anecdotal. In fact, research has revealed a number of proven benefits:

Higher job performance and satisfaction. Simply put, you need things from others to get your work done. Whether it's information, some skill or expertise, an extra pair of hands, or a buy-in for an idea or project, getting what you need enables you to do your job well, and when that happens, you're happier and more satisfied at work.[6]

New-hire success. When starting a new job, you will inevitably need help to navigate your new work environment and understand what's expected of you. Studies show that new hires are less frustrated at work, perform better, and are more likely to stay when they seek and obtain help to clarify job requirements, understand their work setting, and get technical assistance.[7]

Finding jobs—or talent for job openings. Looking for a new job? Or the right person to hire? You're more likely to find them when you ask people in your network for suggestions, recommendations, and referrals. I found my first professional job this way. I was helping a friend and some of his acquaintances move an upright piano, and mentioned that I was completing graduate school and looking for a job in Washington, D.C. Then I asked if anyone had any leads. One of my friend's acquaintances referred me to his old college roommate who ran a consulting firm in the nation's capital. This connection led to a fly-out, an offer, and my job as a project manager in the firm. In the days before the Internet, 50 percent or more of jobs were found via social and professional ties. These ties remain just as important now, even though digital platforms, such as the job-search engine Indeed, are increasingly used.[8] Referrals through social networks produce higher yields than digital search methods, meaning that they result in more actual hiring, and people hired stay longer at their employers.[9]

Learning and professional development. Learning cannot happen in a vacuum.[10] We learn by trying out new skills and ideas and then asking others for feedback about the results.[11] For example, if you want to learn how to give an effective speech, you may be able to prepare and give one on your own, but without feedback on your performance, you'll never know what you need to improve or work on. And most people won't give you feedback unless you ask for it.

Creativity and innovation. Great ideas don't come out of the blue. And innovation is not a matter of luck. We cultivate creativity by asking for and getting information, by exchanging ideas, and by engaging in conversations.[12] For example, when my colleagues and I teach design thinking, we send executives from the comfort of the classroom into the wilds of Ann Arbor, compelling them to approach complete strangers and ask about their experiences with a particular product or service. The execs return with new ideas for their prototypes, as well as the pleasant discovery that most strangers will say yes when asked to participate.

And, armed with great ideas, we need help from others to develop, test, refine, and implement them.[13] Requesting help improves the ability to move ideas from inception to completion.[14]

Managing stress. If you often feel stressed at work or at home, you have plenty of company. Eight of ten Americans (79 percent) say they feel stress every day, and on-the-job stress is the top complaint of American workers, according to Gallup.[15] Research demonstrates that asking for help and support alleviates stress and time pressure—and elevates engagement and job performance.[16]

The benefits of help-seeking accrue to teams and organizations as well. Here's how:

Team performance. Asking for help improves team performance because it enables team members to be more creative, to learn from one another, and to develop a collective understanding of the team's purpose, vision, and tasks.[17] The highest-performing teams cultivate external networks and use them to seek information, feedback, expertise, and other resources.[18]

Cost reduction. The benefits here are significant. Re-

search shows that companies significantly reduce medical, disability, and workers' compensation costs, as well as
experience lower absenteeism and higher productivity,
when their employees voluntarily make use of employee
assistance programs.[19]

Plus, we reduce costs simply by getting to solutions
faster or discovering more economical alternatives. For
example, I once worked with a scientist at Aventis who
needed to synthesize a strain of a particular alkaloid for a
blockbuster drug his team was developing. He was about
to contract with an outside lab and pay $50,000 for the
service. Instead, using the tools in this book, he reached
out to a network of scientists and made a request for a
cheaper alternative. A colleague at Aventis responded to
the request, saying that he had slack capacity in his lab
and could do it for *free,* saving the entire amount that
would have gone to the vendor.

What is telling about this example is that the scientists
were on the *same* drug development team. But because
they weren't in the habit of routinely asking for what they
need, the scientist with slack capacity had no idea that the
other scientist was about to contract with an outside vendor for an analysis that could be done in-house. Voicing
the request made the need known. Once known, others
could respond. And they did.

Encouraged by this success story, other scientists on
the team began making a range of requests, from assistance to screen certain compounds in an enzyme assay, to
permission to observe biological activity assays for a particular project, to help with molecular modeling. When
asked to estimate the total dollar value of the help they
received, the scientists reported immediate savings that

exceeded $200,000—just for this one development team, and in the span of only two and a half hours, the time it took to use a tool from this book.

Productivity and profitability. When help-seeking and giving are the norm in a company, employee productivity is higher and turnover lower.[20] When CEOs frequently ask for feedback about their performance, top management teams become more committed, which in turn improves the financial performance of their companies.[21] And firms are more profitable when they have employees who network broadly and help one another versus firms with employees who focus on individual tasks and individual performance.[22] In the case of the Aventis team, for example, the scientists also reported that the quick responses to their requests saved them more than three thousand hours—time that could now be put toward another drug under development.

Help-seeking improves operational efficiencies because it allows us to find and obtain information, labor, and capital more quickly and reduces duplication of effort. It accelerates the use and flow of an organization's resources. And people are more productive when they don't waste time—and mental energy—by struggling too long on a problem or task before asking for assistance.[23]

It may seem like a paradox, but asking is also the key to *giving*. I first learned this truth decades ago when I started developing tools to enable individuals, teams, and organizations to tap their networks and unlock the wealth of resources around them. Back then, I assumed that getting people to be generous would be the problem. Not so. To my surprise, the real problem was getting people to ask for what they needed. I learned that most people are in fact willing to help—if they are asked. But most people don't ask, and as a result, all those answers, solutions, and resources were being left untouched, unused and wasted—for no good reason.

These early lessons have been reinforced over time by research and the experiences of the many thousands of people around the globe who have used these tools. And these lessons sparked my interest in the reasons why it's so hard to ask for what we need, and motivated my quest to find proven, practical, and effective tools that overcome the obstacles to asking.

Every day I see the benefits of using the methods in *All You Have to Do Is Ask*. I see it in my day job as a professor at the University of Michigan's Ross School of Business, where for more than twenty-five years I have researched, taught, and consulted about generosity, reciprocity, social networks, and positive leadership, and in my role as the faculty director of the Center for Positive Organizations, where I work with more than fifty companies and organizations that are members of our business consortium. I see it as faculty co-director of Leading with Impact, a multi-year partnership between General Motors and Executive Education at the Ross School of Business, where I help leaders from all over the world build networks of giving and receiving that bridge global and organizational silos. And I see it as a strategic advisor and board member of Give and Take, Inc., a company I co-founded with my colleague Adam Grant and others; its mission is to help leaders create robust cultures of reciprocity and collaboration in teams and companies.

Throughout the book, you'll read many of the stories I've learned along the way. You'll learn exactly why so many of us have trouble asking for help, and how to over-come those obstacles. You'll learn simple yet powerful methods to help you craft a request, identify the right person or people to ask, and tap the resources of ever-wider networks. And you'll learn how to use dozens of proven, practical tools that enable teams and organizations to access all the resources they need. I've shared these tools with thousands of executives, managers, and professionals, at companies like Google, Consumers Energy, General Motors, Prudential, Bristol Myers, and Blue Cross Blue Shield. In this book, I show how—regardless of what kind of company you work for, or what position you hold there—you too can adopt these same tools to be more successful at whatever you do. And once you do, anything is possible—even miracles.

CHAPTER 2

A HUMAN DILEMMA:
IT'S HARD TO ASK FOR HELP

When I was a kid, my family took a lot of road trips. My brother, two sisters, and I would cram in the backseat of our wood-paneled family station wagon and try to guess how long it would be before we had to pull over to the side of the road because we were lost. When the inevitable happened, my dad would pull out the map, studying it intently as my mother grew increasingly impatient with his refusal to just ask someone for directions.

Many people joke about how men never ask for directions (or at least they used not to, before the days of Google Maps), but the reluctance to ask for help is not just a male thing. Indeed, help has been called the "original human dilemma."[1]

Based on research that I and others have conducted, plus twenty-five years of business consulting and teaching experience, I've identified eight main reasons we don't give ourselves permission to ask for the things we need. Understanding these obstacles can empower you to overcome, circumvent, or avoid them.

1. WE UNDERESTIMATE OTHER PEOPLE'S WILLINGNESS AND ABILITY TO HELP.

Imagine you're on the streets of New York City when you realize you forgot to make a critical phone call. Now whether or not your best friend gets offered a job depends on you providing a reference within the next half hour. You reach into your pocket or purse, pull out your cellphone, and discover the battery's dead. Bad enough that you forgot to make the call. Worse that you forgot to charge your phone. Your pulse quickens. Now what?

How about asking a stranger to borrow a phone? Would you be comfortable doing that? Most people dread the mere thought of approaching strangers, never mind asking for a favor like borrowing a phone. "Too awkward," you might think to yourself. And plus, what are the chances of someone actually saying yes?

Turns out, much higher than you think. That's what psychologists discovered in a study conducted at Columbia University in New York City (a place not exactly known for the kindness of strangers).[2] Participants had to approach strangers on the street and simply ask, "Can I use your cellphone to make a call?" They couldn't elaborate on why they needed it, or invent some kind of sob story. Nevertheless, much to their surprise, many strangers were willing to oblige: on average, it only took two tries to get a New Yorker to lend them a phone.

In variations of the experiment, other participants had to approach strangers and ask them to fill out a questionnaire, or pretend to be lost and ask to be escorted to a nearby building. Once again, they had to ask only two strangers before one would agree to complete the questionnaire. And it only took an average of 2.3 asks to get a stranger to escort them somewhere.

But here's the really interesting part. Before sending participants out to conduct these experiments, the psychologists had asked them to estimate how many strangers *they thought* they would have to approach before getting a "yes." Turns out, their estimates were way off. They predicted that they would have to ask two or three times as many strangers to get one yes than they actually did.[3]

Finally, the psychologists wanted to know what would happen if the request was even bigger: like for money. They recruited volunteers from the New York City metropolitan area who were participating in Team in Training, a program where people train to walk, run, or bike a marathon or half marathon, or to compete in a triathlon, to raise money for the Leukemia & Lymphoma Society. The only catch is that they have to meet a fundraising goal in order to participate.

When the researchers asked participants to estimate how many people they would have to ask to raise the required funds, they predicted, on average, 210 people. But in reality, they had to ask only 122. And when asked how *much* they thought people would give, they predicted that the average donation would be $48.33—when in fact the average donation was $63.80.

Across all these studies we see a common pattern: we

routinely underestimate others' willingness and ability to help. But the truth is that people actually help one another more often than you might think. In fact, one global Gallup survey found that three of four Americans (73 percent) helped a stranger in need within the month, and that the majority of people in more than half of the 140 countries surveyed have done the same.[4] Moreover, Gallup estimates that, worldwide, *2.2 billion* people helped strangers in just a single month. Another study by an international team of anthropologists and linguists found that of 1,057 everyday requests—whether for some resource, some service, or some support—almost 90 percent were immediately fulfilled.[5] And this high level of helping was remarkably consistent across societies on all five continents.

However, like the participants in those experiments, so many of us assume that others aren't willing to help. We fear we'll be rejected. Or we figure that even if others are *willing* to help, no one will have the time or ability. I've observed this self-limiting belief time and time again in events I've facilitated over the years. Often, someone will take me aside and whisper, "I'm not going to ask for what I really need because I know no one here can help me." Whenever this happens, my response is always the same: "You never know what people know or who they know until you ask. Don't prejudge the capabilities of the group. Just ask for what you really need." And when they do, they are rarely disappointed.

In his autobiography, the storied American inventor, author, and statesmen Benjamin Franklin recounted an episode involving a political rival. Franklin wanted to reduce the animosity in their relationship, but instead of sending a conciliatory letter or gift, he decided to send a request, in the form of a note asking to borrow a rare book the rival had in his library.[6] The book arrived immediately, and after a few days, Franklin returned it, along with a note expressing his gratitude. The result was a complete turnaround in their relationship. "When we next met in the House," Franklin writes, "he spoke to me (which he had never done before), and with great civility; and he ever after manifested a readiness to serve me on all occasions, so that we became great friends, and our friendship continued to his death." Based on his experience, Franklin offered this maxim: "He that has once done you a kindness will be more ready to do you another, than he whom you yourself have obliged."[7]

A charming story, but is there actual scientific evidence to back it up? Indeed, psychologists have found evidence of its veracity. A study found that if you make a request of someone, the person is likely to help you because the person infers an "affiliative motive" behind your request—a desire for a closer relationship.[8] When this happens, the recipient of your request is more likely to feel closer to you in return, which increases their inclination to help you the first time and to continue helping you.

It stands to reason that when a person grants a favor once, you might be emboldened to ask for a second. But what happens when a person declines your request? Would you make a second one in the future? Most people wouldn't dare. But here, too, you would be limiting yourself, unnecessarily. Researchers have found that people *are* likely to respond to your second request, because they feel bad that they refused you the first time.[9]

Many of us also tend to feel uncomfortable making requests of anyone beyond our "inner circle" of family and close friends. But in doing so we vastly underestimate the responsiveness of "weak ties"—our acquaintances and people we don't know very well. Weak ties are extremely valuable because they are the bridges between social circles.[10] Novel information, new solutions to problems, and other resources travel across these bridges. We also vastly underestimate the responsiveness of "dormant ties"—the connections we once had that we haven't maintained. For example, most people wouldn't even consider reaching out to a high school classmate they haven't seen in twenty-five years to ask for a job lead; we assume such attempts to reconnect would be rebuffed, or that our former classmate would resent our reaching out only to ask for a favor. But most people in your past would actually welcome hearing from—and helping—you, according to organizational researchers.[11] The passage of time doesn't erase a shared history of understanding, emotions, and trust.

And reactivating these dormant relationships can be deeply rewarding, in more ways than one. Because you and your high school classmate now live in different worlds, your knowledge and social networks don't overlap as much as they once did. In other words, this person knows things—and people—that you don't. Dormant ties can help you in ways you might not even realize, but you have to ask.

2. WE OVER-RELY ON SELF-RELIANCE.

Consider these two statements. Do you agree or disagree with each one?

- "I would rather depend on myself than on others."
- "I rely on myself most of the time."

If you agree with both statements, you have plenty of company. The vast majority of Americans—85 percent—agree with them, as my team and I learned in four nationally representative surveys we conducted.[12] The value of self-reliance is one of the few that is shared among a wide swath of Americans: across differences in education, income, race, religion, political ideology, and region of the country.

In 1841, Ralph Waldo Emerson captured the essence of this prized human principle in a classic American essay, "Self-Reliance." In it, he advised everyone to "trust thyself," listen to one's own counsel, and avoid dependence on others. We learn the value of self-reliance at an early age, both at home and in school, where we're rewarded for individual achievement and accomplishment.

Then once we enter the workplace, self-reliance becomes a powerful motivator, and one that is regarded as a mark of grit, ambition, and productivity. And while there are certain benefits to being seen as a "self-starter," it's possible to take things too far. If you don't seek advice from your coworkers, you lose valuable opportunities to learn, grow, and develop.[13] And if you don't enlist the help of others to take your innovative ideas from inception to completion and implementation, they'll wither on the vine.[14]

We can take self-reliance too far in our personal lives, too. For example, research shows that failure to seek early treatment for depression, anxiety, or other emotional issues prolongs the duration of the problem and causes more frequent relapses.[15] As many working mothers can attest, trying to "do it all" at home (and at work) leaves them feeling exhausted, resentful, and isolated—all of which can do serious damage to our relationships. On the flip side, the ability to rely on and ask things of our spouse or partner builds trust, commitment, and emotional closeness.[16]

Of course, you don't want help for everything. Getting too much help can rob you of the satisfaction of solving a sticky problem by yourself. But overreliance on self-reliance ultimately dooms you to frustration, and most likely failure.

3. WE PERCEIVE THERE TO BE SOCIAL COSTS OF SEEKING HELP.

Do you worry that asking for help is a sign of weakness? A close cousin of overreliance on self-reliance is the belief that competent people don't ask for help. Organizational psychologists call this the "social costs of seeking help."[17] According to this belief, if you can't figure everything out for yourself, you're telling others that you're weak, lazy, ignorant, dependent, or incapable of doing your job.

The good news is that this fear is largely unfounded. Under the right circumstances, asking for help can actually *increase* perceptions of your competence, according to research by a Harvard-Wharton team.[18] For one, asking for advice says you are confident. It conveys wisdom (you know what you don't know, and you know when to ask). And it says you are willing to take risks. But to make a positive impression, you have to make an *intelligent* request. Asking for advice about a challenging task will increase perceptions of your competence, but asking for advice about a simple, easy, or trivial one will make people think you're either incompetent or lazy. In Chapter 4, we'll take a deep dive into how to make a meaningful and important request.

If we perceive there to be high social costs to asking for help, does that mean that women, who (unfortunately) often have to work harder to earn social capital in the workplace and in society generally, are more reluctant than men to ask for help? The answer is, it depends on what is being asked for, the gender composition of the group, the nature of the task or work, and more. In cultures where men are expected to be more self-reliant and help-seeking is considered an atypical behavior for male leaders, then men will be less likely than women to seek help, fearing that it would impugn their reputations for competence.[19] But the research shows that when working on teams where men are in the majority and when doing stereotypically "male" tasks, such as developing a negotiation strategy, *both men and women* are more likely to ask for performance feedback.[20] Men in male-majority groups doing male tasks are more likely to seek feedback, compared with men in female-majority groups, and much more likely to do so compared with women in female groups with male-oriented tasks. Interestingly enough, women aren't likely to seek feedback in a majority female group that does stereotypical "female" tasks (such as developing a relationship strategy for managing conflict). These gender differences are real, but I've found that the tools in Part II can successfully overcome them, enabling all genders to ask for what they need.

The perceived social costs of asking for help are different across cultures as well. Research shows that Asians, both in their home countries and in the United States, are less likely to request social support for personal problems or feedback about work performance, compared to their Western counterparts.[21] At first, this finding appears to be counterintuitive. Asian societies tend to be collectivistic; the self is viewed as interdependent with others, which might make it easier to reach out for help. In contrast, Western societies tend to be individualistic; the self is viewed as separate and independent of others, which, as we have seen, should make Westerners more reluctant to ask for help. Yet the opposite is true. Why? In an individualistic culture, relationships are viewed as a legitimate means to pursue individual goals. Asking for help from one's social network is acceptable. Asking and even getting turned down don't necessarily harm relationships. In a collectivistic society, however, maintaining social harmony and relationships is a primary goal, and there would be a greater cost to asking for help if it would place a burden on the group or be seen as an attempt to put individual interests above those of the group. To preserve group harmony, then, one might refrain from making requests.[22]

Yet the tools in Part II work as well in Asian contexts as they do in Western ones (and elsewhere). The Reciprocity Ring, for example, is used effectively and successfully in China, Korea, India, Hong Kong, the Philippines, and Singapore—all collectivist cultures. The reason is that these tools make asking for and giving help *group* tasks. They change the rules, so to speak, by making requests obligatory. *Not* asking would be letting the group down.

Preserving group harmony now means making requests—and granting the requests of others.

But is there such a thing as asking for *too much* help? There is. Research on help-seeking reveals that the relationship between help-seeking and performance is not linear—that is, asking for and getting more and more help does not yield ever-increasing performance. Rather, the relationship is curvilinear—an inverted U shape (see below).[23]

Just what does it mean to ask for help "too frequently"? What is deemed "too frequent" is relative; the answer depends in part on your workplace culture and norms.[24] But it also depends on your underlying psychological motivation for seeking help. Psychologists distinguish between two motivations: autonomous versus dependent help-seeking.[25] Autonomous help-seekers aren't asking others to do their work or solve the problem for them; they're asking for help or input in order to solve a problem on

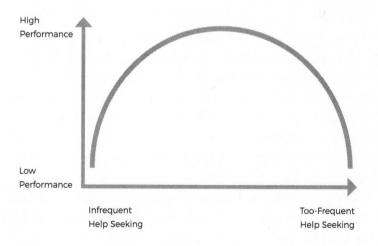

their own. Autonomous help-seekers are motivated to learn and grow. In contrast, dependent help-seekers don't believe they have what it takes to figure something out on their own; they turn to others so they don't have to.[26] Dependent help-seekers don't believe they can learn and grow; they just want the problem to go away.

The key is to always ask yourself: *Why* am I asking for help? Will it help me develop new skills, and learn something new? If the answer is yes, give yourself permission to ask.

4. OUR WORK CULTURE LACKS PSYCHOLOGICAL SAFETY.

It's a sad fact, but in some workplaces, asking for help may have negative consequences. These workplaces lack *psychological safety*—"a shared belief held by members of a team that the team is safe for interpersonal risk taking."[27] When teams lack psychological safety, people are afraid to bring up problems, ask questions, face tough issues, make mistakes, or do anything that makes them feel exposed and vulnerable (like seek help).[28] Add high performance pressure, and people live in a constant state of anxiety— frantic to perform but afraid to try anything new or ask anyone for help.[29]

Psychological safety is essential for people to perform well, especially when performance expectations are high. Based on a study of their own teams, researchers at Google learned that psychological safety is the key to team effectiveness.[30] Other factors matter, of course, such as dependability (getting things done on time, with high standards for excellence), structure and clarity (clear roles, plans, and goals), meaning (work is personally important), and impact (the team's work matters and creates positive change). But far and away psychological safety was found to be the most important—in part because it promotes a culture where people feel as though they have permission to ask for the things they need.

"Asking for and providing help to colleagues is a hallmark of the Google culture," says Kathryn Dekas, People Innovation Lab's lead and senior manager.[31] These behaviors—ranging from "Hey, can I ask you a question?" between teammates at their desks, to posting and replying to questions on an internal discussion group, to directly asking a question to senior leaders at town hall events— "are critical for driving innovation in our products." At the foundation of all these practices, Kathryn observes, "is a feeling of psychological safety—the belief that it's safe to take risks and be vulnerable in front of one's colleagues and teammates."

In Part II I'll talk about tools you can use to help foster this kind of culture in your team or organization by making help-seeking an explicit norm of behavior.

5. THE SYSTEMS, PROCEDURES, OR STRUCTURE OF OUR ORGANIZATION GET IN OUR WAY.

Of course, all leaders want their people to be good organizational citizens, and yet an entire book could be written about all the ways that formal systems, procedures, and practices inhibit behaviors like asking for and giving help. Here, let's look at three common pitfalls: hiring the wrong people, conflicting incentives, and organizational size and silos (in later chapters, I'll discuss what leaders can do to address them).

Hiring the wrong people. What kind of people do you hire in your organization? What selection criteria are used? Often, companies hire solely on individual talent, skills, and experience. The problem is that qualifications like these won't guarantee that a person is collaborative, team-oriented, motivated to help others, and willing to ask for what they need.

So, while hiring for skills and talent is important, it's also important to take values and cultural fit into account. Rich Sheridan, the affable CEO of Menlo Innovations—a leading software firm that produces high-reliability, high-quality, user-centric products—learned that software or technical skills were a poor predictor of fit with Menlo's high-collaboration culture. That's why, as Rich puts it in his first book, *Joy, Inc.,* they look for programmers who have "good kindergarten skills"—people who are respectful, who play well with others, and who share.[32] People with good kindergarten skills gladly help others and freely ask for what they need.

Conflicting incentives. I've yet to meet a leader who doesn't want to create a culture of generosity. But if the incentive system at your organization recognizes only individual achievements, the result is a hypercompetitive culture where asking for—or bestowing—help is not the norm. In extensive laboratory experiments, Cassandra Chambers of Bocconi University and I have confirmed that competitive rankings and individual rewards have a negative effect on cooperation.[33]

Organizational size and silos. It's inevitable that as an organization grows, it splits, divides, and differentiates. When an organization is small, everyone knows everyone; coordination is fast and informal. But rapid growth will quickly turn this tight network into a sprawling array of disconnected groups, units, departments, offices, and divisions. Globalization only aggravates the problem, separating people by distances, time zones, and cultural norms.

The result is an organizational state that is highly siloed. Each silo becomes a separate community with its own goals, objectives, and culture. And asking for and getting what you need is a challenge across this kind of structure. The answer or resource you need is almost certainly somewhere, but it seems impossible to locate, so you don't seek it. As a result, a lot of the resources in your organization are underutilized or not utilized at all. In Part II, I present specific tools leaders need to employ to build a culture of giving and receiving that bridges silos and improves the flow and use of resources.

6. WE DON'T KNOW WHAT TO REQUEST OR HOW TO REQUEST IT.

I've facilitated many events where people are explicitly invited to make a request for something they need—and inevitably, many of them are stumped. Frequently, I hear comments like this one: "I've always wanted to be in a room with knowledgeable, well-connected people and be able to ask for anything. But I can't think of a thing!"[34] There are many reasons people struggle with this. Lack of needs isn't one of them. Not knowing *what you need* is. Most of us are simply not in the habit of articulating goals, or what we need to achieve them. And without knowing where you are going or what you need to get there, it's hard to come up with a request that moves you forward.

The second reason is that even once you know what you need, you may not know how to ask for it. A poorly formulated request can make you seem less competent, and is unlikely to get the responses you need, as people analytics expert Nat Bulkley and I found in our large-scale study of asking, receiving, and giving.[35] And many of us seem to sense this intuitively. In Chapter 4, I provide methods to figure out what you need and how to ask for it, confidently and effectively.

7. WE WORRY WE HAVEN'T EARNED THE PRIVILEGE OF ASKING FOR HELP.

We understand that asking for help is a privilege. And the privilege is earned by giving. Both these statements are technically true; however, if everyone waited to give before they received, then no giving would take place. The way out of this quandary is to recognize that the acts of giving and receiving are a cycle, not a two-way transaction; the objective is to be both a giver and a receiver, in equal measure, over time. Put another way, the "books" can be unbalanced on any given day as long as you're breaking even in the long run. And the books need not be balanced with any single person; rather, they should be balanced across the network of people with whom you interact.

In other words, we should break the link between individual acts of giving and receiving. Giving should mean generously helping others, even—perhaps especially—

when they haven't helped you. And receiving should mean asking for help whenever you need it and accepting it with gratitude. As I describe in the next chapters, there are many ways you can overcome this barrier to asking for help.

8. WE FEAR SEEMING SELFISH.

Finally, we are often reluctant to ask for help because we are afraid we'll be seen as selfishly pursuing our own self-interest at the expense of others. In his 2013 bestseller, *Give and Take,* Adam Grant, professor and management thought leader at the Wharton School, describes such individuals as *takers:* people quite willing to take without giving back or paying it forward, if they can get away with it. Takers, he says, are strategic calculators; they'll help you only if they think doing so will help them more than it costs to help you. Givers, in contrast, generously help without expectations of return. They focus on contribution—the value they create for others by sharing time, knowledge, skills, and contacts.[36]

I first met Adam in 2003 when he entered the PhD program in organizational psychology at the University of Michigan. And how we began to work together is central to the theme of this book.

A few years before Adam went to study there, my wife, Cheryl, and I developed the Reciprocity Ring tool that I mentioned earlier (and will tell you more about in Part II). Cheryl is an organizational development expert and the founder of Humax Corporation, which provides social networking tools and solutions to companies. (Humax is now part of our company Give and Take, Inc.) Back then, we'd come up with the Reciprocity Ring as a powerful and yet simple way for people to tap into a broad network of people willing to generously help one another. The Reciprocity Ring is also what brought Adam and me together.

Occasionally I would conduct a Reciprocity Ring session for staff at the university. One day I was asked to do so but couldn't due to a prior commitment. Unable to bear the thought of simply saying no, I began wracking my brain, trying to figure out who I might ask to run the event in place of me. At the time, I didn't really know Adam, but I did know who he was, and that he had a reputation as a giver; he was known, even then, to always be ready to bestow his time and his knowledge on others. So, I decided I would just go out on a limb and ask him if he would contribute some time to run the event. He cheerfully agreed and recruited a student named Justin Berg (then an undergraduate at Michigan and now a professor at Stanford Graduate School of Business) to assist.

This turned out to be a fortuitous meeting of the minds, and soon we began collaborating on research about the psychological mechanisms behind the Reciprocity Ring and its outcomes. Long story short, my out-of-the-blue request led to a rich professional and personal relationship that lasted long after Adam graduated from Michigan and took a faculty position in the business school at the University of North Carolina. Soon after, he was recruited by the Wharton School, where he became Wharton's youngest tenured professor. Despite his many commitments—as a professor, researcher, and soon, bestselling author—we stayed in touch.

Meanwhile, Cheryl and Humax Corporation continued to provide the Reciprocity Ring to a growing number of companies, business schools, and associations. And I continued to use the tool in my courses, executive education, research, and consulting. As of this writing, over 100,000 people around the world have used this tool, in more than a dozen languages and twenty countries.

Over the years, Cheryl, Adam, and I were asked repeatedly to take the principles of the Reciprocity Ring and turn them into a web tool or app, but each time we concluded that the current technology was not up to the task. But by 2016 the digital revolution had brought platform technologies up to the level where we figured it made sense to try again. So, Cheryl and I assembled a small team, secured initial funding, and developed and tested prototypes. Adam joined us as an advisor and partner, and, with others, co-founded Give and Take, Inc. The prototypes evolved into Givitas—a collaborative technology platform I will tell you more about later in this book. So, in other words, my decision to *ask* a favor of a bright young graduate student had now led not only to a collegial research relationship but also a business partnership.

Our work with Givitas, along with my ongoing consulting and research, has led me to an inescapable conclusion: getting people to "just ask" is the crux of the problem of giving. Adam's *Give and Take* makes a compelling case that being a giver is the road to long-term success. But here's the thing: you can't be a giver if no one is willing to be a receiver. Giving and receiving are two sides of the same coin; you can't have one without the other. You need requests to trigger the cycle of giving and receiving. When people don't ask for what they need, no help is given. In this book, I get to the fundamental problem of getting people to ask for what they need.

In the chapters ahead, I show what you can do individually to make asking a regular habit, while striking the right balance between receiving and giving. And I describe what you can do as a leader of a team, unit, department, or entire organization to create a culture in which people freely ask for what they need *and* generously help one another.

The process begins with an appreciation and understanding of the Law of Giving and Receiving. We're taught that it's better to give than receive, but in Chapter 3 I'll explain why it's best to give *and* receive. Remember, giving and receiving aren't about a tit-for-tat exchange. It's about a higher form of reciprocity—what we call "generalized reciprocity"—that drives the flow of resources through networks. You'll also learn about four giving-receiving styles and their pros and cons, and take an assessment to help you diagnose your style. But no matter what style a person has, anyone can become a generous giver and a frequent requester by using the tools and strategies in Part II of this book.

The chapters in Part II offer proven tools and practices that you can use individually, as a member of a team or organization, or in your role as a supervisor, manager, or leader. What I call "behavior first" is the overarching principle for these tools and practices.[37] The most effective way to change what people think and believe is to first change what they do. As organizational change expert John Shook

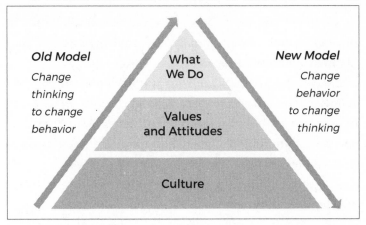

Change behavior to change values, attitudes, and culture.
(Reproduced from "How Culture Changes" by John Shook.)

puts it, "It's easier to act your way to a new way of thinking than to think your way to a new way of acting."[38]

The typical approach to individual and organizational change is to focus on changing what people think and believe, hoping that they will then naturally figure out the right things to do and do them. This old model rarely works. It's hard to directly change people's values and attitudes, and harder still to directly change a culture. But if you get people to try new behaviors—such as experimenting with the tools in Part II—then they'll begin to see the value of them. Over time, they will change their attitude from "asking for help is a bad idea" to "asking for help is essential to my success." And it will change their values from the maxim that "it's better to give than receive" to "the Law of Giving and Receiving is our guiding principle." In short, they will change their minds. Done consistently and repeatedly, and by enough people, these new behaviors can rewire any workplace culture.

Chapter 4 is about how to get started immediately in your personal and/or professional life. It guides you through a step-by-step process, starting with how to figure out what you need and how to translate your needs into requests. Next, it guides you through the process of tapping your networks to figure out whom to ask. Finally, it covers how to handle the occasional rejection, turning a "no" into a new ask.

Chapter 5 moves to the level of teams: how to create psychologically safe places in which team members are enabled to ask for and give help. Building an effective team begins with setting the stage for success, including selecting people for it who are inclined to be giver-requesters and establishing norms that foster psychological safety, especially when asking for and giving help. This chapter describes how a team leader can reinforce these norms by modeling them, and by making giving and asking a part of everyone's job description. This chapter then provides several tools that you can use to establish asking and giving routines in teams and groups.

Chapter 6 moves up another level, focusing on asking across boundaries, like the barriers between organizational silos or organizations, as well as those between us and the world's networks. Asking across boundaries expands the giving-receiving network, virtually guaranteeing that you'll find the answer or resource you need. In this chapter, I describe proven practices that bridge boundaries, as well as digital technologies that do the same.

Chapter 7 emphasizes the importance of recognition, appreciation, and rewards. When used properly, they strengthen the tools and practices I described in the preceding chapters. I'll explain how to reinforce asking by rewarding those who ask, how to make asking for help an explicit performance competency, and how to design compensation systems that marshal and reward collective improvement efforts.

By the end of this book, you will have learned the *All You Have to Do Is Ask* process and how to implement it in your personal and professional life. You will have learned how to implement and benefit from the Law of Giving and Receiving—individually, and in any group, team, or organization.

Before we continue, however, I want to emphasize this point: this book is not a license to be a taker. Far from it. It's an invitation—and a how-to manual—for participating in the exchange of resources across our personal, business, and professional networks. Asking for help is the essential ingredient because it initiates the process of giving and receiving. The secret to a culture of contribution is giving yourself and others permission to ask.

SUMMARY

A request for help starts the cycle of giving and receiving, but eight barriers stand in the way of asking. Some are psychological, such as being too self-reliant or feeling that you haven't earned the privilege of asking for help. Some are erroneous beliefs, such as thinking that others are unwilling or unable to help, or that you may be perceived to be incompetent if you ask for help. Sometimes the context is a problem, such as workplaces where it feels unsafe to take risks, or organizational systems, procedures, and practices that get in the way of asking for what you need.

And sometimes it can be as simple—and as easily solvable—as not knowing what to ask for or how to ask. In the next chapters, I describe what you can do to surmount these barriers.

REFLECTIONS AND ACTIONS

1. Of the eight reasons why it's hard to ask for help, which ones stand out as the biggest obstacles for you? Why?
2. Are your beliefs your biggest obstacles? (Reasons 1, 2, 3, 8.) If so, continue reading to change your beliefs.
3. Is your biggest obstacle that you don't know what to ask for or how to ask? Or that you haven't earned the privilege of asking? (Reasons 6 and 7.) If so, then proceed to Chapter 4 and follow the advice there.
4. Is your context or situation the biggest obstacle? (Reasons 4 and 5.) If so, then jump ahead to Chapters 5, 6, and 7.
5. Keep a personal development journal as you continue reading this book. Jot down your reflections, ideas, and actions. When you're ready, share with others what you've learned and insights you've had.

CHAPTER 3

THE LAW OF GIVING
AND RECEIVING

n the run-up to the Summer Olympics in Rio de Janeiro, Italian restaurateur Massimo Bottura hatched an idea to rescue the enormous amount of food wasted by the thousands of athletes, coaches, and officials who lived and ate in the Olympic Village and use it to feed healthy meals to the homeless in Rio.[1] So, he and Brazilian chef David Hertz founded a nonprofit, Refettorio Gastromotiva, to do just that. They leased a plot of land and built a restaurant that uses rescued food to make and serve more than one hundred meals a day to the homeless. The restaurant is still open to this day, years after the closing ceremonies of the Olympic Games, and Bottura eventually began similar ventures in London, Melbourne, the Bronx, and elsewhere.[2]

This inspiring initiative is the perfect illustration of how we usually think of giving and receiving: a transfer of resources from those who have to those who have-not. It fits what we've been taught since childhood: it's nobler to give than to receive. This view is extolled in over twenty-four of the world's religious and wisdom traditions.[3] Billions of people globally give their money, time, assistance, and talent to help those in need, according to Gallup's global engagement study.[4] And we see it manifest across our cultures, too; as one example, here in the United States, helping others is the most common theme in college commencement speeches.[5] In short, giving is widely recognized as a virtue, all over the world.

The belief that giving is better than receiving extends beyond the charitable acts of giving food to the hungry, money to the penniless, shelter to the homeless, or relief aid to victims of natural disasters or war. In our careers and in our workplaces, we consider helping others to be a virtue—a sign of a good organizational citizen—but we are uncertain about receiving.

I agree with the spirit of giving. I believe that we have a responsibility to help those in need. And I believe that generosity is both a virtue and its own reward. But might there also be virtue in receiving? The Fetzer Institute, a nonprofit foundation that promotes individual and community health and wholeness, articulated this question well, writing that "we tend to bestow and project all sorts of virtues onto the giver but are largely silent about the virtues of the receiver. We all have heard many times 'It is better to give than to receive.' At first blush, this makes great sense. We want to live in a culture of givers. But though we want to encourage people to give, do we mean to say it is wrong or 'less good' to receive?"[6]

I'll leave this question for philosophers to debate. However, I've learned that while it's generous to give, it's even more generous to give *and* receive. The twin acts are two sides of a single coin. There is no giving without receiving and there is no receiving without giving. And it's the request that starts the wheel turning. The circulation of resources through our personal, professional, and business networks depends as much on our seeking help as it does on our providing it.

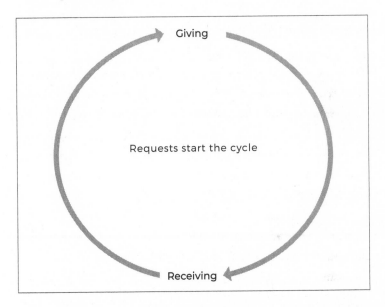

If you think about the most well-regarded and productive people you know, you'll realize they are those who generously help others *and* who ask for what they need. Adam Grant calls these people "otherish"—they combine concerns for others and concerns for self.[7] These are the people who fuel the cycle of giving and receiving.

In this chapter, I make the case that asking for help is as important as giving it: what I call the "Law of Giving and Receiving." I describe the four general styles of giving and asking, and help you determine which category you fall into: Are you an overly generous giver, a selfish taker, a lone wolf, or a giver-requester? These are not inborn traits, but rather choices you can make about how you want to operate in the world. In Part II of the book I'll offer a suite of tools you can use to change your behavior in the desired direction and also provide guidelines for living the Law of Giving and Receiving.

FOUR TYPES OF GIVERS AND REQUESTERS

Think of giving and asking as two dimensions. One dimension represents low to high frequency of giving; the other represents low to high frequency of asking. Where are you on these dimensions? To find out, take this quick scientific assessment. You can also take the assessment on the website for this book (allyouhavetodoisask.com). There, you will be able to see how you compare to others.

Asking-Giving Assessment

Instructions: Below are different ways that people can ask for and provide help. Please think about your own experiences, both at work and outside of work, over the past month or so. Then indicate how often you did each action.

Asking	Not at all	Once a month	2–3 times a month	Weekly	2–3 times a week	Nearly every day	More than once a day
I asked for information.	1	2	3	4	5	6	7
I asked for help with a task.	1	2	3	4	5	6	7
I asked for emotional support.	1	2	3	4	5	6	7
I asked for advice on a personal matter.	1	2	3	4	5	6	7

Asking	Not at all	Once a month	2–3 times a month	Weekly	2–3 times a week	Nearly every day	More than once a day
I asked for a lead or referral.	1	2	3	4	5	6	7
I asked someone to sponsor me or my team.	1	2	3	4	5	6	7
I asked a friend or colleague to introduce me to someone.	1	2	3	4	5	6	7

Giving	Not at all	Once a month	2–3 times a month	Weekly	2–3 times a week	Nearly every day	More than once a day
I provided information.	1	2	3	4	5	6	7
I helped someone with a task.	1	2	3	4	5	6	7
I provided emotional support.	1	2	3	4	5	6	7
I gave someone advice on a personal matter.	1	2	3	4	5	6	7

Giving	Not at all	Once a month	2–3 times a month	Weekly	2–3 times a week	Nearly every day	More than once a day
I provided a lead or referral.	1	2	3	4	5	6	7
I sponsored a person or team.	1	2	3	4	5	6	7
I introduced a friend or colleague to someone I know.	1	2	3	4	5	6	7

Scoring: For the Asking scale, add up your choices for the seven questions, and then divide the total by 7 to get your average Asking score. Follow the same procedure to get your average Giving score. Record each score separately.

Today's date: _____

My average ASKING score: _____. My average GIVING score: _____.

Comparisons: In our survey of 465 working adults who represented a wide variety of roles and industries, the average Asking score was 2.53, and the average Giving score was 3.21. Only ten percent of these working adults could be classified as Giver-Requesters, with both Asking and Giving scores greater than four.

Here are some questions to think about as you contemplate your results:

1. How do your scores compare with our sample of working adults?
2. Is your Giving score greater than four? Why or why not?
3. If your Giving score is low, what specific actions can you take to increase how often you help others?
4. Is your Asking score greater than four? Why or why not?
5. If your Asking score is low, what specific actions can you take to increase how often you make requests?

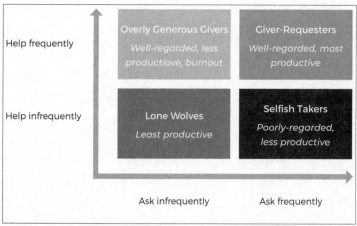

Source: Scale developed by Wayne Baker and Hilary Hendricks at the University of Michigan, May 2019. (Copyright © 2019 by Wayne Baker and Hilary Hendricks)

Each of the two dimensions is continuous, but it's help-ful to think of them in terms of four main types or styles: overly generous givers, selfish takers, lone wolves, and giver-requesters. Let's explore each one.

Overly Generous Givers

If you're a giver, says Adam Grant in *Give and Take,* "you simply strive to be generous in sharing your time, energy, and knowledge, skills, ideas, and connections with other people who can benefit from them."[8] Implicit is the as-sumption that benefits eventually will come to the giver, however indirect the path may be. As I wrote in my second book, *Achieving Success Through Social Capital,* "By prac-ticing generalized reciprocity—contributing to others with-out worrying about who will help you or how you will be helped—you invest in a vast network of reciprocity that will be there when you need it."[9]

Sometimes, however, givers take their generosity too far. For seven years I taught two sessions a year for Lead-ing Women Executives, a private nonprofit career develop-ment program for high-level women executives in major corporations. In my session on strategic relationships and networks, I always emphasized the importance of generos-ity and contributions to others. And year after year, many participants would protest, saying that they already help others and freely give of themselves. Plenty. And they feel depleted.

These executives were suffering from "generosity burn-out."[10] Inevitably, during our discussion, they would have a breakthrough about why they *never ask for help.* They were so focused on giving, and afraid to appear weak or incompetent, that they were reluctant to make their needs known. But in doing so, they were denying themselves the power of generalized reciprocity, allowing their energy to be depleted, and frustrating all the people they have helped and who want to help them in return.

The overly generous giver is a seductive role. They get to enjoy what economists call the "warm glow" of giving.[11] They bask in the admiration of others. The positive feedback they get for their good deeds boosts their self-esteem. The problem, however, is that by failing to make themselves vulnerable by disclosing what *they* need, overly generous givers miss out on the ideas, information, opportunities, leads, referrals, and other resources they need to be successful. And the research backs this up. For example, one study in a telecom firm found that those employees who gave a lot but didn't get a lot were well regarded by their peers, but were less productive because they didn't receive the help they needed.[12]

In the extreme, the overly generous giver style produces more than generosity burnout—it can be hazardous to your health and well-being. Giving too much and not taking care of yourself is called "dysfunctional generosity."[13] A related phenomenon is "professional compassion fatigue"— common among healthcare providers, such as hospice and palliative care nurses—which can lead to extreme stress, mental and physical exhaustion, insomnia, and more.[14]

If you fall somewhere in this overly generous giver category, know that it is possible to change. Later in the book I'll offer some battle-tested strategies to help you jumpstart the process of learning to ask for what you need.

Selfish Takers

Selfish takers, on the other hand, take the advice to "just ask" too far, and are prone to forgetting or neglecting their obligations to others. As the name implies, they are so self-focused that they rarely, if ever, repay the generosity bestowed on them. Or as a friend of mine who worked at IBM Consulting described them: "Sponges! They suck in everything around them and don't give a drop back!" Selfish takers may benefit in the short run, but eventually people wise up and stop helping them. Just as we reward generosity, we punish stinginess.[15]

Don't get me wrong: in some situations, we may have to take much more than we give. New hires, for example, may require help at work long before they can offer it. And people who are down and out may have no choice but to accept help in order to get back on their feet. These are not the people we are referring to when we talk about selfish takers.

The good news is that even the most selfish takers will give—in the right circumstances. Controlled experiments that I've conducted with Sheen Levine of the University of Texas bear this out.[16] First, we measured participants' baseline values around giving and receiving, then we placed them in laboratory groups and had them play what's called the "indirect helping game" (think of paying it forward). Real money was at stake. We controlled whether decisions to give to others were announced to other participants, or made in private. Sure enough, we found that those with taker values were more likely to be generous when their actions were public than when their actions were private. Givers, however, gave no matter what.

Adam Grant and I took a similar approach when we put givers and takers together in the Reciprocity Ring. Adam and I had a friendly bet: he thought that takers wouldn't give, under any circumstances, and I thought that they would. To find out, we measured participants' giver-taker values, had them participate in the Reciprocity Ring, and then counted how many offers of help each person made. The results? We were both right. Takers did give. But they gave a lower rate than givers.

Why did takers give at all? When giving is out in the open, takers "gain reputation benefits for being generous in sharing their knowledge, resources, and connections," says Adam. "If they don't contribute, they look stingy and selfish, and they won't get as much help with their own requests."[17] I call this the "potluck principle": a selfish taker will bring a dish to a potluck dinner because not doing so would be too conspicuous, not to mention embarrassing. Takers, in other words, exhibit what I call "enlightened self-interest," meaning they give when they believe it is in their long-term self-interest. Many tools I present in Part II of this book are designed to incentivize takers to give by making giving and receiving public.

Lone Wolves

Lone wolves are rugged individualists. Because they value self-reliance, they rarely, if ever, seek help. Nor do they tend to give it. Some people intentionally choose the lone-wolf work style, thinking (erroneously) that the path to success is to put your head down, focus on your tasks, and grind it out—alone. They view success as a race to the top—so why would they slow down or stop to help the other runners catch up?

Lone wolves are poorly regarded because they don't help others, and at the same time, their performance is impaired because they don't get the inflow of help and resources they need.[18] Moreover, by staying to themselves they become disconnected from the people around them. This social isolation delivers a double whammy, as numerous studies clearly document that social connection and rich social capital improve performance, whereas isolation and poor social capital impair it.[19]

Social isolation is often a symptom of a dysfunctional workplace. My wife, Cheryl, once worked as a senior analyst for a national association in the healthcare insurance field. In that organizational culture, everyone was expected to be self-sufficient. Employees were expected to stay at their desks and accomplish their tasks quietly and on their own, and asking for help was seen as a sure sign that you were incompetent and couldn't do your job. Even casual conversation was considered wasting time. Like many of her colleagues, Cheryl soon left for a job in a different organization. Association leaders were puzzled about why the organization had so much trouble retaining employees.

Beyond workplace outcomes, being a lone wolf takes a toll on health, happiness, and well-being.[20] Studies have even found that social isolation and loneliness in older people is one of the biggest predictors of functional decline and death.[21] And among young adults, the feeling of social isolation can "impair executive functioning, sleep, and mental and physical well-being."[22]

Despite the way our culture perpetuates the myth of the rugged individual, it's better to be an overly generous giver, or even a selfish taker, than a lone wolf; even a taker is connected and not alone in the world.

Giver-Requesters

Giver-requesters live and breathe the Law of Giving and Receiving. By giving help, they earn a reputation for generosity; by seeking it, they receive the things they need to succeed. Numerous studies show that this is the balance we should strive to achieve. For example, in the study of a telecom firm, the most productive and well-regarded employees were those who frequently gave help and who frequently received it.[23]

Companies that live the Law of Giving and Receiving reap the benefits as well. IDEO, a design firm renowned for sustained creativity and innovation, owes much of its success to a robust "culture of helping" in which knowledge workers gladly share what they know and ask for help as soon as they need it.[24] And Menlo Innovations, the software firm I mentioned in the previous chapter, integrates giving and receiving into the fabric of work. These examples are just a few of many that show how giving *and* receiving enable you and those around you to innovate, to execute, and to create value.

Remember, the Law of Giving and Receiving is not about direct reciprocity, as in: "I help you and you help me." It's about helping others regardless of whether they helped you before or will ever help you in the future, and it's about asking for what you need when you need it.

This doesn't only benefit your work, but also your day-to-day satisfaction and overall well-being. In one study, Adam and I measured participants' emotions, positive and negative, before and after they engaged in the Reciprocity Ring. We learned that when people gave *and* got help, they experienced an increase in positive emotions and a decrease in negative ones. That's because giving help produces the warm glow of giving, while receiving help produces the "warm and fuzzy" feeling of gratitude.

Acts of both extending generosity and graciously receiving it are investments in a network of giving and receiving. And over time, those investments will yield powerful returns.

Guidelines for Giver-Requesters

Here are four guidelines to keep in mind as you live the Law of Giving and Receiving:

1. Give without strings attached; give without expectations of return.
2. Give freely but know your limits; avoid generosity burnout.
3. Don't hesitate to ask when you need help, but avoid dependent help-seeking.
4. Take a long view. At any point in time, you may be giving more or receiving more; in the long run, strive to be a giver and a seeker.

SUMMARY

Giving and receiving is a cycle that begins with an ask. The Law of Giving and Receiving dictates that you should strike a balance between giving help and requesting it. Overly generous givers help too much; as a result they suffer impaired productivity, generosity burnout, or worse. Selfish takers freely ask but neglect the obligation to help, and their reputation suffers. Lone wolves are the worst off; they don't participate in the cycle of giving and receiving at all. Those who are well regarded and the most productive freely help others and also freely ask for help when they need it. These giver-requesters are esteemed for their generosity *and* get the inflow of resources they need to achieve superior performance.

REFLECTIONS AND ACTIONS

1. To what extent do you practice the Law of Giving *and* Receiving?
2. Which of the four types are you—and why? Does it aid achieving your goals?
3. Does asking for what you need take you out of your comfort zone? If yes, why?
4. What do you need—right now—to solve a problem or make progress on a task or assignment? Ask for it.
5. Look around you. Is there someone you can help? Is there someone in need?
6. Find a way to help that person. If you can't help directly, make an introduction to a person who can.

ASKING FOR
(AND GETTING)
WHAT YOU NEED:
A TOOLKIT

CHAPTER 4

GET STARTED NOW: FIGURING OUT WHAT YOU NEED AND ASKING FOR IT

"You learn to ask for help."

That's Ji Hye Kim's answer when asked the best business lesson she absorbed on the way to becoming a managing partner at Zingerman's Community of Businesses in Ann Arbor, Michigan.[1] With more than sixty-five million dollars in annual sales, Zingerman's includes a dozen award-winning businesses in the artisanal food and hospitality industry. But Ji Hye (pronounced "Gee-Hey") didn't begin her career in the food business. Growing up in Seoul, Korea, she loved the traditional cuisine but never thought of food as an option for a career. She first came to Ann Arbor as an international student at the University of Michigan, earning a degree in Economics and Political Science. After graduation, she took a job at an outsourcing firm in New Jersey that handled human resources, accounting, and other administrative tasks for hospital clients. Her hard work, long hours, and ability to learn on the job paid off, when, just three years after college, she was offered and took a six-figure job as an executive at a similar New Jersey company.

With this illustrious start to her career in business administration, how—and why—did Ji Hye end up back in Michigan, working in the food business? Love, of course. Ann Arbor was where she met her future husband. When they married, he stayed in Ann Arbor at a job he enjoyed while she continued to work in New Jersey, flying in to see him every weekend. Ji Hye was making good money but was increasingly disillusioned with her job and tired of being separated from her husband. Eventually, she saved up enough money to quit, moved permanently to Ann Arbor, and gave herself time off to ponder, "What do I *want* to do with my life?"

One weekend, Ji Hye and her husband threw a party for friends and hired the nearby Zingerman's Deli to cater it. She marveled at how good the food was and how happy the employees were. Around the same time, she read a *New York Times* article about Zingerman's twenty-fifth anniversary, talking about the company's international reputation, unique ways of organizing, and visions to create new types of food-related businesses. After Ji Hye found an *Inc.* article that called Zingerman's "the coolest small company in America," she decided she wanted to work there. She applied for a job at the deli and at the bakehouse. When the bakery rejected her due to lack of relevant experience, she was disappointed. But after the deli interviewed her for a job in the catering department, had her work a trial shift, and then rejected her, she called the hiring manager and made the first of what would be many asks on the way to what would become a fruitful partnership: "Would you please let me know what I could have done better," she asked, adding, "because I will apply again." The manager couldn't come up with anything specific she had done wrong but said he would think of her the next time a position opened up. And he did. Soon after, Ji Hye was working a $9/hour job at the deli, selling hundreds of cheeses and olive oils from around the world. Deli retail "was a good stroke of luck," Ji Hye recalls, "because it kept up my curiosity." "Know the product" is one of Zingerman's mantras, and she had a lot to learn about cheese making, olive agriculture, food chemistry, growers and suppliers, and more. She loved the positive energy at Zingerman's, and working thirty to forty hours a week, it felt like a vacation after seventy-plus hours a week at her old job in New Jersey.

After a few years, however, Ji Hye began to get restless. "I had too much time on my hands," she recalls. She'd gained a new appreciation for food and cooking while working at the deli, so she decided to try to start experimenting in her own kitchen. She soon perfected the recipe for the dumplings her family made back home in Korea, and began selling them at a friend's Japanese restaurant. Ji Hye then learned about Zingerman's new-business development model, whereby employees can propose business ideas and receive the training, experiences, and education required for a successful business. Those who make it through open a new business under the Zingerman's umbrella.

Together with a fellow employee, she tested some recipes with gatherings of friends. People seemed to love the food, but Ji Hye knew she still had a lot to learn about running a restaurant. And she understood that if she wanted help, she was going to have to ask for it. At one point, she organized, cooked, and hosted a large party, and asked guests to send her feedback about the dishes she had served, then went back and improved the recipes. Then she asked a friend who ran tastings at Zingerman's Deli to run one for her. She even asked the friend to distribute and collect feedback sheets at tastings and analyze the data. When she ran low on funds, she approached one of Zingerman's founders, Paul Saginaw, and asked for a company credit card to pay for future expenses as well as an accountant to keep the finances in order. Paul agreed. "Asking was easy," Ji Hye says, "but you have to know what you need, what resources are out there, and who to ask."

During this time, Ji Hye was building her network in the vibrant local food scene. At one point, a friend who owned a hot dog cart suggested she try opening an Asian street food cart as the next step. She loved the idea, but didn't have the manpower or the cash to make it happen. So, Ji Hye invited Paul and his partner, Ari, to work with her, and when they agreed, she asked them to find and purchase a used cart, then find a place in Ann Arbor to park it. "I wasn't shy about asking them to pay for stuff," she recalls. "In return, I was going to make full use of every opportunity." Prior to starting the food cart business, Paul suggested that she and her business partner go to Asia to research food. Ji Hye asked Zingerman's to pay for plane tickets to Japan, Taiwan, Korea, and Hong Kong, and asked friends and acquaintances in these countries if she could stay with them.

Upon their return, she and her partner set up the food

cart. After the first season, her partner decided it wasn't what she wanted to do, so she and Ji Hye parted ways. Ji Hye continued with the food cart for three more seasons. Realizing that she needed to up her game, Ji Hye asked to work in the prep kitchen at Zingerman's Deli and then at the sandwich line, where she could learn how to produce food in volume. She asked to apprentice as a sauté cook at Zingerman's Roadhouse, a full-menu restaurant in Ann Arbor. Finally, she decided it was time to get some experience as a "stage"—essentially, an unpaid intern—at some high-end Korean restaurants. She identified one in New York City, sent a cover letter, and received no response. She emailed to follow up; still no response. So, she bought a plane ticket and showed up at the restaurant, asking them to take her on. They agreed to let her work for one day. At the end of her shift, she asked to be allowed back. "If it's not too much trouble, I'm here for two weeks and I'd like to come back. I'll take out the trash, cut vegetables, whatever you want. Is it okay for me to come in?" She spent two and a half weeks there.

After almost ten years at Zingerman's, she opened Miss Kim, a high-end Korean restaurant. My family and I've eaten there many times, and to say the food is fabulous is an understatement. It took a lot of hard work, and a lot of asking for favors, but Ji Hye's dream had finally come to fruition.

"The most transformational thing I learned," Ji Hye explained, "was [that] being a partner . . . is not about relinquishing control, which had been my biggest concern. I realized that I'm not an expert at everything. I learned that it's about being both independent and functioning within a community at the same time. It's about making better decisions by having access to more information and exper-tise. . . . [It means] that you're committing to being a part of the community, engaging in dialogue and giving and accepting help when needed."

In other words, Ji Hye learned to live the Law of Giving and Receiving.

Like Ji Hye, you might dream of someday running your own business. You might be on the path to a leadership role in your organization. You might be a new hire striving to fit in, get along, and learn the ropes. You might be moving toward a promotion, a new job, or even an entirely new career. You might be an entrepreneur looking for the next Big Idea. You might be on a personal journey of self-discovery and development. You might be seeking new ways to make positive contributions within your family or community.

Whatever path you're on, one thing is certain: learning to ask for what you need—whether it's advice, mentorship, information, materials, referrals, funds, or just a friendly ear—will help you get closer to your goal. Remember, the things we need are often much more attainable than we think, and people are generally much more generous with their help than we tend to believe. And yet, even once we recognize this, we still struggle. Why?

Sometimes the problem is that we don't know exactly what we need. We might be aware that we're stuck or stalled but unsure what it would take to get moving again or pick up speed. For example, when a colleague of mine relocated from New York to San Francisco for a new job, he left a community of friends and family for one where he knew nobody.[2] His new job kept him busy, but he felt lonely and didn't know what to do about it—or what kind of help to ask for.

Other times, we might know exactly what we need, but have no idea who to ask for these things. And sometimes we know what we need and who can give it to us, but simply aren't sure how to articulate the request in a powerful way.

In this chapter I offer a simple step-by-step process to help you figure out *what* to ask for, *who* to ask, and *how* to ask in a way that will set you up for a yes. Underlying these methods, however, is the recognition that asking for what you need is a privilege, not a right. This chapter is about asking, but it embodies the spirit of the Law of Giving and Receiving. That means making the commitment to give help as well as to seek and accept it.

DETERMINING YOUR GOALS AND NEEDS

Begin with the end in mind. By that I mean, before you can determine your needs, you first have to understand what you are trying to accomplish or achieve. Having meaningful goals isn't just useful when it comes to identifying needs, it's actually a prescription for satisfaction and happiness in life.[3] Goals provide structure and meaning, purpose and control. Making progress toward meaningful goals gives you confidence. And pursuing goals often requires you to engage other people and develop positive relationships—which produce happiness.[4] But not all goals are created equal. The ones most likely to bring you happiness are intrinsic, meaning you find them inherently interesting, inspiring, and energizing, rather than simply a means to an end.[5] And they are authentic, meaning that they represent your passions, interests, strengths, and values, rather than being goals that were chosen for you—by parents, by peer pressure, by your boss, by some felt sense of what you "ought" to do.

My MBA students often struggle with staying true to their authentic goals when they recruit for jobs. Consider, for example, Lauren, a business student who excelled at economics and finance.[6] As graduation day approached, she was feeling peer pressure to take a job on Wall Street, even though she wanted to do nonprofit work. After two unhappy years at a financial firm, however, she got back on track and left to take a low-paying job at a nonprofit in Washington, D.C. Eventually, she returned to school, earned a master's degree in Public Policy, and is now happily employed as a manager at Teach for America.

It's easy to see how reconnecting with our authentic goals can motivate us to do whatever it takes to attain them. There will be times, however, when you will have to pursue goals that don't feel authentic, or that you don't feel committed to. These may be part of your formal job description, or something that your boss hands you. When this happens, it's helpful to keep the endgame in mind— that is, what you want to accomplish long-term. Perhaps a long-term goal is promotion to a senior position in the company. If successfully completing the less-than-energizing project your boss dumps on your desk will help you get there, then you can see the assigned goal in a new light: a stepping-stone on the path to promotion. From this perspective, the assigned goal is easier to own because you are committed to the long-term goal you freely chose: promotion to a senior position in the company.

What are the most meaningful goals in your life right now? What do you need to achieve them? You may know your answer immediately. If so, jump ahead to the next section (Translating Your Needs into SMART Requests). If not, here are exercises that will help you figure out what your goals are—and what you need to get there. You can choose any or all of these methods—but you may want to try the quick-start method first and go from there.

(1) QUICK-START METHOD

Consider and complete these five sentence starters. If you get stuck on one, just move to the next.

1. I am currently working on

   _____

   _____

   _____

   and I could use help to

   _____

   _____

   _____.

2. One of my urgent tasks is to

   _____

   _____

   _____,

   and I need to

   _____

   _____

   _____.

3. I am struggling to

_____

_____

_____,

and I would benefit from

_____

_____

_____.

4. One of the biggest challenges in my life is to

_____

_____

_____,

and I need advice on

_____

_____

_____.

5. My biggest hope is to

_____

_____

_____,

and I need

_____

_____

_____.

Chris White, managing director of the Center for Positive Organizations, used this Quick-Start Method as he was making his transition to the private sector after seven-plus successful years leading and growing the Center. "*I am currently working on* building a consulting practice," he wrote, "*and I could use help to* decide on the best business structure as it grows. Specifically, I could use help figuring out the pros and cons of a partnership, LLC (limited liability company), S corporation, and a C corporation."[7] Once he'd identified that need, he realized that he should ask a few successful entrepreneurs to share their insights, and also consult an accountant for tax advice and a lawyer for legal guidance.

(2) ARTICULATING YOUR GOALS

If you've completed one or more sentence starters, pick the one that energizes you the most and move ahead to the next section (Translating Your Needs into SMART Requests). If you found yourself struggling to complete the above sentences, however, you may have to do a little more legwork. Turn to the goal worksheet on the next page. Pick a category that feels most urgent to you—whether it's your job, career, business, health/fitness, family, spiritual/religion, or community. Write down your most important goal in that area, and follow these easy steps:

Describe the Goal: Provide concrete details about what you are working toward, and be sure to include *why* the goal is meaningful and important to you. For example, when Larry Freed, CEO of our company Give and Take, Inc., did this exercise, he chose "business" as his category and "develop metrics for knowledge collaboration" as his goal. Here's how Larry described that goal: "You cannot manage what you do not measure. We want to develop a set of metrics that enable people to measure the strength in knowledge collaboration at an individual level, team level, and organizational level. The reason why this is important is that it will enable our clients to improve knowl-

Category: _____	To accomplish this goal, I need:
	1.
Goal Name: _____	
	2.
Description:	
	3.
	Etc.
Due Date: _____	
	Possible needs: information, data, reports, leads, advice, ideas, materials, referrals, support, etc.)
Metric: _____	

Make copies of this worksheet if you want to work on more than one category or goal.

edge collaboration in their organizations, and for us to demonstrate the value of Givitas."

In guiding people through this goal-articulation exercise, I've noticed that the "why" is often left out; when people state a goal like "grow my business" or "spend more time with my spouse or partner," people think that the "why" goes without saying. But the truth is that sometimes even we don't know what our "why" is until we try to articulate it.

Reflecting on the why is critical because it provides clarity about the goal. And it may remind you of why the goal is so meaningful and important, which not only becomes a source of energy and motivation for you, it also helps to energize and excite those you share it with. By the same token, reflection might help you realize the goal isn't that authentic to you after all, and that the best course of action is to abandon it.

Date the goal. Pick a specific time by which you hope to attain or accomplish your goal. Even if the date is just a wish or best-case scenario, writing it down forces you to think through the process. You may discover that the goal would be far less daunting if broken up into steps or intermediate goals. Larry picked May 1, which was twelve weeks from the date he completed the goal worksheet. This was an ambitious but doable time frame.

Choose a metric. Finally, you need a metric—an objective measure that will tell you clearly whether you've accomplished your goal by the date you specified. Otherwise, it's like running a race without a finish line—you never know if you won or not. Larry specified two related metrics for his goal: to have created a system of measurement for Givitas that a) works across different sizes and types of organizations, and b) can provide value to our clients by allowing them to benchmark their organizations as compared to others.

Determine your needs. Once you have named, described, dated, and provided a metric for your goal, the next step is to determine what resources you need to achieve or make meaningful progress toward it. For example, Larry needed to recruit a variety of organizations to use Givitas so that he would have a large and diverse data set with which to develop the Givitas metric. He specified the number, types, and sizes of the organizations he would later ask to participate.

It's worth noting here that resources come in many forms, from the tangible (like a material resource or a loan) to the intangible (like a referral or introduction to someone). What you need depends on what you are trying to accomplish. Here are some examples. Note, however, that these do not come close to exhausting all the possibilities of what you might ask for.

- *Information:* facts, knowledge, or data about something or someone. Examples: (1) "At work, our goal is to redesign our incentive plan to make it more effective. Does anyone have information regarding effective incentive plans?"[8] (2) "I'm developing a new algorithm for optimizing wholesale prices for sales to our customers, and I need data on pricing history to test and refine it."
- *Advice:* an informed or expert opinion about what should be done about a particular issue, problem, person, or situation. Examples: (1) "I'm going nowhere in my job and career, and I need advice from anyone who has been stuck and figured out how to get unstuck and move forward." (2) "After thirty years, we are retiring and selling our business. We need advice about how to do it, pitfalls to avoid, and how to price the business."
- *Recommendation:* endorsements of a person, place, thing, etc. Examples: (1) "We're replacing our in-house, in-person management development program with a digital platform, so our employees can participate at their own pace. Could you recommend an effective one?" (2) "I'm applying for a new job. Would you write a letter of recommendation for me?"
- *Referral:* connecting one person to another for information, advice, services, etc. Examples: (1) "We are planning our annual all-employee conference. Can you introduce me to any speakers who are experts on the topics of leadership, team dynamics, career development, or related issues?" (2) "My daughter is struggling in middle school and I think she might have a learning disability. I need to be connected with an expert in the area who can conduct a professional evaluation."

- *Financial Resources:* cash, budget commitment, loan, donation, grant, charitable contribution, etc. Examples: (1) "Our team has completed our budget for next year, and we need to bring in 10 percent over last year's annual budget if we are going to meet our sales goals. We are looking for surplus funds." (2) "Our company has created a fund to support employees pursuing research or patents. The money is a grant, not a loan you have to pay back. We are seeking applicants now."
- *Human Resources:* salaried staff, hourly workers, temporary help, interns, volunteers, etc. Examples: (1) "We are adding a second shift to our production line and we need to hire new workers with relevant experience." (2) "With two people on our team planning to take short-term leaves, we need to replace them with temporary hires."
- *Participation:* recruiting people to join a group, or show up for a program or activity. Examples: (1) "I am preparing for the CFA L1 (Chartered Financial Analyst Level 1) in June. If someone is interested in joint study and/or discussion/review for the exam, let me know." (2) "We're putting together a task force to tackle the problem of product defects in our manufacturing process. Would you join it?"
- *Physical Resources:* materials, supplies, facility space, offices, plant, equipment, and so forth. Examples: (1) "I'm about to contract an outside vendor to perform a chemical analysis. I'm looking for a lab in our company that might be able to do the analysis instead and that would be a cheaper option." (2) "With all the new hires, we are bursting at the seams and need additional office space. Modular or temporary space would be fine."

Whatever your need, be specific. Then move to Translating Your Needs into SMART Requests.

(3) YOUR VISION

I've run the Quick-Start Method and Goal Worksheet exercise with hundreds of people, so I've seen how effective they are in bringing clarity about what you need. If you completed one or both, you are ready to translate your needs into requests. However, there is one more powerful approach to figuring out your goals: visioning. This is more time-consuming than the other two methods, but many people have found this extra step to be worth the investment of time and thought.

Visioning is a method for determining the outcome you want. It's not about *how* you will attain a goal (we'll get to that shortly), it's *what* success looks like. It isn't a mission statement or a strategic plan; it's not a short phrase, slogan, or tagline. In a way, a vision is a story. Not in the sense of fantasy or fiction, but in the sense that it requires imagery, and imagination. It's not about wishing for something to happen, it's about getting clear on what you intend to make happen. Typically, a vision is written as a narrative, in the present tense (even though it's about a future date). You can craft a vision for your career or personal life, for a new project, product, or an entire company. I've seen visions for just about everything—family vacations, retirement plans, and more.

For example, when I became chair of the Management & Organizations (MO) department at the Ross School of Business, one of the first things we did was collectively write a detailed vision for the department that we wanted to be five years later. The vision covered four areas: Great Research, Great Teaching, a Great Place to Work, and an Active Part of Our Communities.

The idea and practice of visioning originated with Ron Lippitt, a social scientist from the University of Michigan Institute for Social Research. Back then, he called it "preferred futuring."[9] In studying many real teams Ron observed a common pattern: those who leapt right away into identifying problems and debating solutions lost energy quickly and didn't make much progress. So, he tried an experiment. He had some teams develop visions of the positive future they wanted. Having this mental picture of what success would look like at a future date—and the process of creating it—increased energy, excitement, and motivation, which enabled them to address their current problems and make more meaningful progress.

I've learned that vision should also be (1) inspiring, (2) strategically sound, (3) documented, and (4) communicated.[10] "Communicated" is where asking for help comes in. When you share your goal, you are asking for help in achieving it. Once people know where you are trying to go, you'll be amazed at how readily they'll offer ideas, suggestions, contacts, and other resources to help you get there.

TRANSLATING YOUR NEEDS INTO SMART REQUESTS

It was the summer before my tenth wedding anniversary. At the time, my wife and I were fans of *Emeril Live,* the popular cooking show starring celebrity chef, restaurateur, and cookbook author Emeril Lagasse. Each episode was filmed live in front of a studio audience, and guests who sat up front got to sample Emeril's fare. One evening, while watching the show, I asked my wife what she would like to do to celebrate our upcoming anniversary. Without hesitation, she replied that we should go to a taping of *Emeril Live* to celebrate our milestone. I gulped, worried that I had bitten off more than I could chew. In my mind, we were more likely to win the lottery and get struck by lightning on the same day than we were to get seats in the studio audience for this show.

If I was to even have a fighting chance of scoring two tickets, I was going to need to ask for help.

But how? My first step was to translate that need into a request. Though at that point I had no idea *who* I would ask for help with this mission, I first needed to get clear on *how* I would ask.

A well-formulated request satisfies SMART criteria: Specific, Meaningful, Action-oriented, Realistic, and Time-bound. You may have heard SMART defined as Specific, Measurable, Assignable, Realistic, and Time-related.[11] I define *M* as "Meaningful" because explaining the "why" of a request gives it power. You may also have heard *A* defined as "Achievable." I prefer to define *A* as "Action-oriented" because action is how you obtain the resource you need to achieve or make progress toward a goal.

Specific—People often think that making broad, general requests is effective because it casts a wider net, but in fact a specific request yields more help than a vague one, because details trigger people's memory of what and who they know in a way that a general request does not. The vaguest request I ever heard was made in an event I was running, by an executive from the Netherlands, whose request was for "information." That was it. One word. "Information." When I asked him to elaborate, he replied, "That's all I can say. It's confidential. I need information." Unsurprisingly, he didn't get any help that day (though he did end up offering help to others).

Meaningful—Why is the request important to you? When others know *why* you are making the request, they are more motivated to respond. They empathize with you. Unfortunately, people often leave out this criterion when making requests. They assume that the importance of the request is self-evident or obvious. But it never is. You must explain why the request is meaningful and important *to you.*

When I planned to make my request for two tickets, I knew I had to explain why those particular tickets were so meaningful and important. It wasn't an "Oh, wouldn't it be great to see a taping of *Emeril*?" kind of request. A request with a compelling "why" motivates others to respond. It provides energy and inspiration. The *why,* says Simon Sinek, inspires people to act.[12]

In some situations, the *why* isn't just about what's meaningful to you. For example, if you are making a request of your boss, how does your request fit with his or her goals, objectives, and priorities? How does your request serve the larger interests of the organization? If you're an entrepreneur pitching investors, you wouldn't just say you want a million dollars, you would explain why you are seeking capital, what problem you/your company is solving, why you are the right person to solve it, and why their investment will pay dividends for everyone involved. Whatever request you are making, be sure to consider the context and make the "why" about more than just you.

Action-oriented—A request is not the same as a goal. A goal is an end state, a destination. A request is a call to action on the road to your destination. People often make the mistake of stating goals or describing a situation and assuming that others will intuitively know what actions need to be taken. That's rarely the case. In a career coaching event I once attended, one participant said that his request was for "help switching careers from finance to marketing." But no one was sure what he was asking for. Did he want someone to make a referral? Did he need advice about making the switch? Only after a lot of questioning did the group learn that what he really wanted was to sit down and talk with someone who works in marketing so that he could get a better sense of what the career actually entails.

Realistic—Your request can be big or small, but it has to be realistic. I'm not saying you should make requests only when you are certain they can be fulfilled; I'm saying that the request has to be strategically sound. Consider my request for two tickets to be on *Emeril Live*. It was a serious long shot, but within the realm of possibility (two tickets to the moon, in contrast, would not be realistic).

Time-bound—Every request should have a due date. How could anyone help with the two tickets, for example, without knowing when I needed them? Many people don't like putting a due date to their requests because they're afraid they might seem too demanding. In my experience, however, this fear is unfounded. Actually, people prefer a deadline because it allows them to evaluate whether or not they will be able to follow through by the date, and/or enables them to carve out time for whatever the request in-volves. Vague deadlines like "sometime this quarter" or "next year" invite inaction or procrastination; they don't motivate people to respond. If your request is urgent, say so. But even if it's not urgent, you still need to specify a due date.

IT'S ALL ABOUT NETWORKS: FIGURING OUT WHO TO ASK

Once you know what you need, and have crafted the re-quest you want to make, the next step is figuring out *who* to ask. Sometimes you will know exactly who the right per-son is and you can direct your request accordingly, but other times you need to do some legwork. The key is to figure out "who knows what" (sometimes called the "knowl-edge network") and "who knows who" (the "social net-work")[13] in order to find someone who has the expertise or resource you need—or who can identify and point you toward someone who does.

Generally, when we need something, we start with the people we know. But while going to your small circle of friends may feel most comfortable, the reality is that many resources reside outside your circle. And when it comes to ideas and information, we run the risk of groupthink and conformity of opinion when we rely only on our close circle of connections.[14]

Going beyond our inner circle can feel a bit overwhelm-ing. With all the people in the world, where do we even *begin* looking for someone with access to the specific re-source or information we need? One great place to start is close to home—or rather, close to work—by consulting company personnel profiles and knowledge databases (short summaries of members' expertise), or by looking up colleagues' LinkedIn profiles.[15] From there, you might branch out to industry blogs, such as the Manufacturing Innovation Blog at the U.S. Department of Commerce National Institute of Standards and Technology or the Harvard Business Review blog. Also consider reaching out to professional societies and associations, such as the Society for Human Resource Management or the National Academies of Sciences, Engineering, and Medicine.

Once you find the person you think might have what you need, reach out, even if this person is a very loose connection (such as a friend of a friend)—or a total stranger, for that matter. A European director of a professional services firm described the time he was preparing to pitch a new client in Europe and needed some background.[16] He asked his staff and others in his office, but no one had the information he needed. So, he consulted the firm's knowledge database, found a person in Australia who had worked with this client, and called him—even though they were complete strangers. The Australian responded promptly, and they arranged a conference call for their teams the next day. Reflecting on the incident, the European manager said, "I expect that when I need information I can send out a call to the system, to the company as a whole, and get a response back . . . you get reciprocation from the system."[17]

Dormant ties—like former colleagues or classmates, teachers and coaches, old friends, and even Facebook friends you haven't been in touch with in years—are another commonly overlooked source of help. Thanks to social media, connections you haven't maintained can be more easily reactivated than ever, and these connections can be like a portal to a whole new world of social and knowledge networks. Research shows that while business executives *prefer* to make requests of people with whom they have active relationships because it's more comfortable, dormant ties are actually more *valuable* sources of help because your knowledge and networks don't overlap as much as they once did.[18] Be sure to also tap your *dormant* ties, not just your current relationships.

If you've exhausted all these connections and are still stuck, it's time to move to second-degree connections. When my son was in high school he joined the track team. He wanted to learn how to throw the discus and shot-put, so he asked me to find a private coach. I didn't know anyone with these particular skills, but I did know a fifth-year senior on the University of Michigan women's cross-country team who had taken one of my courses. I figured that she would know throwers on the Michigan team, so I emailed her and asked. Within forty-eight hours, she put me in touch with a recent graduate who was an All-American thrower. A week later, he was coaching my son.

Innovation expert and thought leader Jeff DeGraff regularly uses this two-degree approach when he seeks resources for the Innovatrium, an idea laboratory, innovation institute, and community for innovators that exists in part to grant people access to a diverse and wide range of experts for their projects and assignments. "We often don't know who the expert is," Jeff told me, "but we know who to ask *to find the expert*." Indeed, Jeff and his colleagues used this process with remarkable success more than 180 times in a single year.[19]

In one instance, Jeff was helping one of the world's largest pharmaceutical companies redesign their drug discovery process. This process is extraordinarily complex and highly regulated, which meant that they "needed to find someone who not only understood the current state-of-the-art of drug discovery—with all of its obstacles and serpentine twists and turns—but also emerging technologies and methodologies that could be used to circumnavigate them," Jeff says.[20] So, he called an old friend in the university's development office who worked with faculty at the College of Pharmacy and explained exactly what he needed. Jeff's friend promptly connected him with a young Chilean professor who had created an experimental method of discovering new compounds, and who was more than happy to come to Innovatrium and discuss his research with the pharma company's senior scientists.

Intuitively it makes sense that the more people you share your request with, the more likely you are to find someone who knows somebody who can help. This was certainly true for me in the case of the *Emeril* show. Remember, at first I didn't have a clue who to ask. Not only did I not know anyone with access to tickets, I didn't even know someone who knew someone with access to tickets! Soon, however, a golden opportunity fell into my lap. Three months before our tenth anniversary, I was scheduled to lead an orientation session on building social capital for the University of Michigan business school's incoming MBA class. The event was held in Palmer Field at the university, where the over 550 students gathered in huge circus-like tents while the faculty's remarks were piped in on jumbotrons. Well, I thought to myself, if there ever was a chance to put my request to a large and captive audience, this was it! During my event, I made my request via jumbotron, explaining the whole story—that we were great fans of the show and how, one night when watching an episode, I asked my wife what she wanted to do for our anniversary. I then made my request to be on *Emeril Live* in time for our anniversary.

Even I couldn't believe what happened next. Over the course of the afternoon, several students came up to me with a lead. One had a friend who was dating Emeril's daughter and offered to connect me (true story, but they broke up soon after, so the connection didn't happen). Another student and his wife were friends with Emeril's segment producer on ABC's *Good Morning America,* where Emeril occasionally hosted a cooking segment. That student introduced me via email to the producer, who cheerfully arranged for us to meet Emeril himself.

We flew from Detroit to New York City, spent the night at a hotel, and the next morning took a cab to ABC studios, where we met Emeril on the set. To our delight, he was friendly and down-to-earth (and we even caught a glimpse of actress Glenn Close, who happened to be one of the show's guests). Okay, so we weren't on *Emeril Live,* I thought to myself, but we were about as close as we might hope to get. Then, just as we were about to leave the studio, Emeril's producer stopped us. In her hands were two VIP tickets to the filming of *Emeril Live* later that day. So, not only did we get to go to the taping—we got to go as Emeril's guests!

Just when I thought it couldn't get any better, we learned that they were taping the upcoming Valentine's Day show that evening, so I decided that during the show I would surprise my wife on air with a gift of a ring. Turned out that our moment was captured on camera, and in addition to airing as part of the show, a brief clip of us embracing became the trailer for Emeril's Valentine Day's program for two years in a row.

It couldn't have been a more perfect anniversary celebration. Nor a more perfect example of how when we just ask, amazing things can happen.

But what if you don't happen to have the opportunity to speak in front of hundreds of well-connected MBA students, the way I did? I'm willing to bet you still have ready-made opportunities. Perhaps you can make your request in a regular staff meeting, or bring it to a community group that you are a member of. And, luckily, we live in an era that is abundant with digital technologies that provide access to large audiences, including an array of question-and-answer sites such as Quora (general public, all topics) or Stack Exchange (for programmers and software developers). Then there are platforms like Nextdoor (a neighborhood-based social networking platform), Task-Rabbit (an online marketplace to find help for everyday tasks), HomeAdvisor (digital marketplace to find pre-screened home improvement and maintenance professionals), Upwork (a global marketplace for freelance services like web design, copywriting, and programming work), and many other portals to expertise and services. And most companies provide messaging platforms like Yammer, Jive, Slack, or Chatter, which make it easy to reach a large swath of colleagues at once (though these platforms work best when the group or company is small, or it already has a positive culture in which it is psychologically safe to make requests). In the chapters ahead, I give examples of other collaborative technology platforms and tools that work quite well.

MAKING REQUESTS: THE ART OF THE ASK

You've determined your needs, translated them into SMART requests, and identified who to ask. Now it's show-time. But first you have a few choices to make. If you are making a request of a particular person, will you call a meeting, make an appointment, or just drop by? Will you text, phone, or email? Email and text have their place, but it's easy to overestimate their effectiveness. In fact, research shows that a face-to-face request is thirty-four times more effective than an email message![21]

Or maybe you just try to run into the person. For example, after I completed my PhD at Northwestern University, I took a job at a management consulting firm in Washington, D.C., where it was impossible to get a meeting with the senior partners. I soon discovered, however, that if I timed it right, I could catch one of them at the elevator, ride with him to the first floor, and even walk with him to his car in the parking garage. During these couple of minutes, I had his undivided attention and could present any request I needed to make.

So, your face-to-face request could be quick, informal, and casual. "Hey, can I ask you a question?" "Could I run something by you?" "Do you know where I can find X?" It could be made by a formal presentation, as when an entrepreneur pitches a prospective investor, or via a written report, as when a manager submits a formal budget request.

Or anything in between. Making a request is more an art than a science; it's up to you to decide how, where, and when. Here are some general guidelines you can adapt for your situation, the request you are making, and the person or group you are tapping for help.

Where:

- Adapt to the communication style and media preference of your audience. Does the person prefer verbal or written communication? If verbal, do they prefer face-to-face interaction, a phone call, or video conferencing? If written, do they prefer text, email, LinkedIn, or a hard document?

When:

- You want to make the ask at a time when the person can listen to your request and thoughtfully consider a response. For example, be sensitive to the person's situation, responsibilities, and work load. If they are stressed out, working on a short deadline, or going through difficulties in their personal life, wait until a better time to ask.

How:

- Use SMART criteria. Specific, meaningful, action-oriented, realistic, and time-bound; be sure to address each component, even if briefly.
- Be direct and authentic. Don't start with an apology like "I'm sorry to ask, but . . ." Don't underplay the request. Say "This won't take a moment . . ." only when it takes a moment. Don't use psychological tricks like "You know I'd do this for you, so I know you'll do it for me. . . .").

- Accept a rejection gracefully, even if the negative response is delivered ungracefully.
- Accept a positive response with appreciation and gratitude.
- Close the loop by letting the person know what happened after you received the help you requested. What was the outcome or result?

TURNING THE OCCASIONAL "NO" INTO A (SUCCESSFUL) NEW ASK

As we saw in Chapter 1, people are more likely to respond to your requests with a "yes" than you might think. But occasionally, you will get a no. Then what? What does "no" really mean, anyway?

Consider the story of Jia Jiang, a young immigrant from Beijing, China, who aspired to be the next Bill Gates. At age 30, he quit a six-figure job at a Fortune 500 company to found a start-up that he was confident would create the next killer app.[22] He tapped his life savings, hired software engineers, and started building prototypes. Four months in and already running out of money, he pitched an investor who had previously showed some interest. Soon after, Jia got an email. The investor wasn't interested after all. The answer was no.

Jia was so devastated by the rejection that he struggled to press ahead. He knew there were plenty of other investors out there, but he was so plagued with self-doubt and insecurity, he couldn't handle another rejection. Eventually, he came to realize that his *fear* of rejection was worse than the sting of rejection itself. Determined to overcome this fear, he embarked on a journey that he dubbed "100 Days of Rejection." Each day for a hundred days, Jia made a silly, ridiculous, or outrageous request that he assumed would be rejected. In the same way that one might conquer a fear of heights by going skydiving or climbing to the top of the Empire State Building, Jia figured that surely getting a hundred requests denied would desensitize him to rejection (you can read about what happened in his book *Rejection Proof* or his blog 100 Days of Rejection Therapy). On day one, he asked to borrow $100 from a complete stranger. The answer was no. On day two he asked for a free "burger refill" at Five Guys. No again. In short, the experiment worked: most of Jia's one hundred requests were rejected, just as he had hoped.

He also learned a few things along the way.[23] First was that a "no" almost always contains information that can help you hone the request, increasing your chance of success the next time you ask. Jia learned that asking a simple "Why?" after an initial rejection could turn a no into a yes—or at least provide more information that could lead to a yes. One day he bought a ready-to-plant rosebush, went to a stranger's house, knocked on the door, and asked the man who answered if it was okay for Jia to plant it in the yard, free of charge.[24] The man said no. "No problem," Jia said, "but may I ask why?" Turns out that the reason wasn't because the guy didn't trust Jia or thought the request was weird. He simply didn't plant flowers in his yard because he knew his dog would destroy them. Then the man suggested that Jia try the neighbor across the street, who loved flowers. Jia asked her, and she not only said yes, but seemed genuinely delighted by the unexpected gift of a new rosebush for her yard.

Jia also learned that rejection isn't personal. It's an opinion, not the objective truth about the merit of an idea. In fact, a rejection may say more about the rejector than the requester or request, and you generally don't know the reason behind the "no" you get: maybe the person wishes to help but is unable, the timing isn't right, or they are just having a bad day. Plus, rejections are often subjective judgments and prone to error. Did you know, for example, that J. K. Rowling's first *Harry Potter* book was rejected by publishers twelve times?[25] Like Rowling and many other famous authors, artists, and inventors whose work and ideas were repeatedly rejected—until they weren't—Jia learned that rejection can be a powerful source of motivation and resolve to keep asking until you get what you need.

SUMMARY

Asking for what we need doesn't come easily for most of us. Asking is a behavior that must be learned. It requires three steps: determining your goals and needs, translating needs into well-formulated requests, and figuring out whom (and how) to ask. You can use one (or all) of three methods to determine your goals and needs: quick-start, goal setting, and visioning. Once you've identified your needs, use SMART (specific, meaningful, action-oriented, realistic, and time-bound) criteria to translate those needs into effective requests. Figuring out whom to ask requires you to know "who knows what" or "who knows who." When you don't, you can consult directories, profiles, or bios, reach out to a dormant tie, or try to find secondary connections. Finally, you can broadcast your requests to groups, either in-person or via social media and social networking sites. And remember that rejection is just an opinion. And opinions change. In other words, you *can* find ways to turn a no into a yes.

REFLECTIONS AND ACTIONS

1. Which method worked for you—quick-start, articulating your goals, or visioning?
2. Which goal did you pick and why?
3. What request did you make? Did you follow the guidelines?
4. When you made your request, what happened? Why?
5. If you were rejected, how could you turn the "no" into "yes"?
6. Share what you learned with a trusted friend, colleague, or advisor.
7. If you don't have an inspiring vision of the future, begin the process of writing one. It's one of the surest ways of living the life you want.
8. Return to and use this chapter whenever you feel stuck and don't know what to ask for.

CHAPTER 5

TOOLS FOR TEAMS

When I completed my doctorate at Northwestern University, I didn't become a business school professor right way. Rather, I decided to get more real-world experience, taking a job as a senior associate in a management consulting firm in Washington, D.C. I stayed at the firm for several years, eventually becoming a managing partner and vice president. It was a fast-paced, high-expectations, long-hours kind of place. Our team motto seemed to be ready, fire, aim. Whenever we landed a new project and assembled a team for it, we would dive in and immediately get to work. It was as though there was no time to spare for things like getting to know our teammates or establishing positive norms and habits. The results were, to put it charitably, variable. Sometimes teams succeeded, but many other times they failed, leaving members discouraged, emotionally bruised by the experience.

Back then, I thought failure was the result of bad chemistry, the wrong mix of people. Now I realize that a major factor was our haste in getting started. The start of a new team project is a time of high stress for its members; everyone is rushing to solve problems and produce results without enough preparation or thought.[1] That is why it's so critical to set the stage first.[2]

Stage-setting includes establishing explicit norms around giving and receiving. High-performance teams depend on the free flow of ideas and knowledge, collaborative problem solving, and mutual aid and assistance. It's therefore critical there be explicit norms empowering team members to ask for what they need: from creative suggestions, advice from more experienced team members, and help fixing a problem or removing roadblocks, to a helping hand with heavy workloads, connections to people and resources outside the team, and more.

In this chapter, I describe how to set team norms and routines that give people permission to ask. Next I provide several tools to ensure a seamless flow of knowledge, ideas, and resources within and across teams small and large. These tools have been stress-tested everywhere from Fortune 500 companies like Google, Nationwide Insurance, Southwest Airlines, and DTE Energy to medium and small firms like IDEO and Menlo Innovations, to nonprofits like the Detroit Institute of Arts, Center for Positive Organizations, and DoSomething.org. They are designed to be applicable in all industries, all types of companies, and teams of all shapes and sizes.

Before we continue, it's important to recognize that no effective tool is ever one-size-fits-all. Every team will need to adjust, customize, and adapt these tools to fit its business needs, its culture, and its people. Note, too, that these tools do not cover all the requirements of effective teams.[3] But they will give you a good head start.

Finally, getting the most out of these tools and routines requires you take a learning orientation.[4] By that I mean being motivated to learn new skills, ideas, and tools *and* being open to learning from experience. So, a learning orientation means being willing to experiment, knowing that there will be mistakes or misfires along the way, and it also means being resilient, bouncing back, and not letting a mistake or failure derail you. Of course, these strategies and tools alone don't guarantee a team's success. But they do set the stage for it.

SETTING THE STAGE FOR TEAM SUCCESS

Setting the stage creates the conditions in which team members feel safe to bring up problems, make mistakes and talk about them, share good and bad news, make requests for what they need, and reciprocate by helping others. All of this begins with selecting the right people.[5]

Selecting the Right Members for the Team

When selecting people for a team, the typical checklist emphasizes human capital, like skills, work experiences, and accomplishments—the types of information captured in company personnel databases, résumés, or LinkedIn profiles. Of course these things are critical. You need people with the right set of skills, talents, strengths, and experiences for the job at hand. But you also need generous givers who freely ask for help. In other words, look for people who exhibit concern for others' welfare, an inclination to help, and who are ready, willing, and able to ask for what they need.

One way to spot giver-requesters is to weave the questions from the assessment I provided in Chapter 3 into your interviews with candidates. Another way is to adopt or adapt the hiring practices used at places like Southwest Airlines. Widely renowned for its positive workplace culture, Southwest is now the largest domestic carrier in the United States.[6] And people flock to work there; the company receives an average of 960 résumés a day and hires only 2 percent.[7] When considering applicants, Southwest emphasizes "hiring on values," including "a servant's heart," which Vice President and Chief People Officer Julie Weber describes as "the ability to put others first, treat everyone with respect and proactively serve customers."[8] At Southwest they don't just talk about hiring for values, they actually screen for them as part of the interview process, with questions like, "Describe a time when he or she went above and beyond to help a coworker succeed."[9]

To this I would recommend adding a question like: "Tell me about a time when you ran into a problem and you reached out for help." If a blank stare is the answer, you've learned something important!

Once you've selected the right members for the team, the next step is to begin the process of building a culture where asking for and receiving help becomes the norm.

Building Psychological Safety

What happens when nurses and respiratory therapists don't speak up when they see a possible medication error or other cause for concern? Patients die. That might sound melodramatic, but medical errors are more common in healthcare teams where it's unsafe to speak up, question, or disagree with the medical doctors in charge.[10] And healthcare professionals (who aren't doctors) are more likely to speak up when doctors are inclusive, invite contributions and questions, and appreciate those who speak up.[11]

Most situations are not that dire. But whenever teams lack psychological safety, or "the shared belief that the team is safe for interpersonal risk taking,"[12] members won't feel as though they have permission to ask for the things they need to be successful. Kyle (not his real name) learned this the hard way.[13] An experienced fund-raiser, he was hired by a prominent nonprofit organization to work in a team of fund-raisers to write proposals and administer large grants. He had a lot to learn about fundraising in this institution, but he was a quick study and asked for help when he needed it. Everything seemed to be going well, so he was surprised when, at his first-year performance review, his manager said, "If you're going to ask for help on proposals, why are you taking lunches and leaving work on time?" "Okay," Kyle thought to himself, "I guess I will never ask for help again. Why should I, just to get reprimanded?" From then on, Kyle sat at his computer from 8:00 A.M. to 4:30 P.M., leaving only to go to the bathroom. He didn't take lunch or breaks. "Even on days when I have four or five proposals due, and I can see that my peers are just killing time, I won't ask for help."

And as Kyle soon learned, his boss's comment stemmed from a larger attitude that pervaded the organizational culture. In staff meetings, for example, Kyle said that people are shut down when they ask questions or raise an issue. "By looks, sounds, or words," he said, "we are made to feel that what we have to say is not important." Staff meetings devolved into one-way information dumps. It wasn't safe for people to speak up.

Psychological safety is essential for creating a culture of asking, giving, and receiving. When people feel safe, they ask when they're stuck and need help, or when they make a mistake and need help fixing it, or when they're struggling under a heavy workload and need help. In fact, research conducted at Google indicates that psychological safety is the *key* to team effectiveness more generally.[14] Of course, other factors matter, too, such as dependability (getting things done on time, with high standards for excellence), structure and clarity (clear roles, plans, and goals), meaning (work that is important to people personally), and impact (the team's work matters and creates positive change). But based on a comprehensive study of their own teams, researchers at Google concluded that psychological safety is, far and away, the most important factor in a team's success.

HOW SAFE IS YOUR TEAM?

If you make a mistake, is it held against you? Can you freely ask for help without fear of criticism or ridicule?

If you want to quantify your feelings, take the short assessment in the appendix. This diagnostic was developed by Harvard Business School Professor Amy Edmondson, who pioneered research on psychological safety in teams. You can take the assessment yourself, or you can ask a few trusted teammates to take it with you as well. With data from the assessment in hand, return to this chapter to figure out a plan of action to improve psychological safety.

Taking time to set the stage before the team dives into work is key to establishing psychological safety. If the team is new, give people ample time to get to know one another on a personal basis. If some people work remotely, be sure to use Skype, Zoom, Google Hangouts, or other videoconferencing platforms. The simple fact of seeing one another personalizes the experience.

If you're at a loss as to what to talk about, try using the FORD guidelines to steer that conversation: Family, Occupation, Recreation, and Dreams. Give each person enough time to talk about each topic, and for others to ask follow-up questions. This exercise should be a conversation, not a series of presentations. It's often a good practice for the team leader to model the process by being the first to ask a question, or share personal details. To break the ice, I like to ask "What is something that is not generally well known about you?" (Adding "and please keep it legal" always gets a chuckle.) If every team member approaches this conversation with an open mind, and the spirit of sharing, you will have made a solid investment in team cohesion, spirit, and psychological safety.

This is also a good time for the team leader to emphasize and discuss the importance of psychological safety, and the norms of freely asking for and giving help. At this point, the team could also decide which tools they want to use toward that end. The team leader should not impose choices on the group; rather, the team should discuss each tool and come to a consensus about which ones are right for them.

At Google, setting the stage often includes something known as a "premortem," a management practice originally developed by Gary Klein.[15] "Premortem" (which means "before death") may seem like an ominous moniker, but in fact it's a positive practice that helps teams deliver on their mission. As a senior Googler explained to me, a premortem involves getting a team together before a project begins to brainstorm all the ways it might fail. Engaging in a premortem, I've found, is liberating. It frees up people to ask questions, discuss problems, and sets the expectation that people should not stay quiet if they see things going in the wrong direction as the project unfolds. I like to couple a premortem with what I call a "previtam" ("before birth"), a quick exercise designed to help the team paint a vision of what success looks like: both for the current project and for the team more generally.

The world-renowned design firm IDEO is known for its robust "culture of helping."[16] And, as Heather Currier Hunt, IDEO senior global director of Learning & Development, observes, IDEO has a culture of helping precisely because they have a culture of *asking* for help. Central to that culture is the use of a process they call "flights." Whether the project at hand is short-term or long-term, client-facing or internal, technical or artistic, every team at IDEO uses this three-step process on a regular basis to foster clear and effective communication and collaboration across the team.

The first step, the preflight, is a time to set the stage: to discuss hopes and fears, set norms around asking for (and giving) help, and establish expectations about responsibilities, schedules, levels of experience, and so on. Someone new might say, "I don't know much about this topic, so I will be in learning mode. I will need you to be patient with me and bring me along as I learn. I'll be asking a lot of questions and will need your help!" Another might say, "I have little kids and I have to leave at four-thirty every day, but you can count on me being totally dedicated when I am here." The preflight, says Heather, brings clarity about what they need as a team, and as individuals, to be successful.

Midflight, as the name implies, is a check-in midway through the team's journey. "It's a forcing function," Heather says, "that gets the team to talk about dynamics." Of course, team members should ideally be asking for help throughout a flight, but the midflight check-in is a time to review the team's progress, figure out what additional or new resources are needed, and reaffirm the team's norms and expectations about asking for and giving help. This is also a good time for the team to reflect on what is and isn't working, and adjust if necessary.

Post-flight occurs after the team's work is done. It's a time of "catharsis, celebration, and synthesis," says Heather. In other settings, this practice might be called an "after-action review," or a postmortem. Regardless of the language you chose to use, this is the time to discuss learnings, and give and receive feedback on what could have been done better.

The post-flight discussion can be uncomfortable if things didn't go as planned. And if things went well, the post-flight can be rushed, as people are eager to move on to the next project. But it's important to take the time to consider and discuss how well the team lived the Law of Giving and Receiving. It can help to have a quick, anonymous survey prior to the post-flight session, asking questions like: How safe did you feel asking for what you needed? Did you feel you gave more than you got from the team? Did anyone lack help or resources? Then, during the post-flight, you can review the results from the survey and use them as a basis for discussion. Remind everyone that post-flight is a learning opportunity, not a forum for blaming or finger-pointing. Focus discussion on lessons learned for the future: What should we continue doing, and what should we do differently to make sure the team has all the resources needed for success?

The Leader's Role

When Dr. Salvador Salort-Pons became the director, president, and CEO of the Detroit Institute of Arts (DIA), he startled his leadership team by initiating a new practice: asking for help on a regular basis. Despite his team's initial surprise, this practice caught on quickly, in large part because Salvador employed it himself. "I like to ask for help and advice," he told me.[17] "While I have a curatorial background and a business degree, there are some areas of the operation of the museum that I am only superficially familiar with. I bring in the experts in those areas and ask for their advice. I'm not afraid to show that I don't know something. It's a better place to start [when] you recognize in front of others that you don't know something and to ask those who do to help you understand," he explained.

Salvador's experience highlights a key point: the team leader plays a vital role in establishing psychological safety. If a leader's words and actions don't communicate that it's safe to ask for help, few—if any—team members will do so. That's one reason why, Heather Currier Hunt described to me, it's common to see an IDEO leader reach out and say something like: "Help! Does anyone know anything about this topic?"[18] It's important for leaders to freely admit when they don't know something, and ask for what they need.

As a leader, says Amy Edmondson, you need to "acknowledge your own fallibility" and "model curiosity by asking a lot of questions." It's also critical to normalize mistakes, or, as Amy puts it, "frame work as learning problems, as opposed to execution problems."[19] This doesn't mean mistakes should be ignored or swept under the rug. To the contrary, they should be acknowledged as part of the learning process. After all, if people fear that mistakes will be met with derision and blame, then they will hide them, when what you want is for people to openly disclose what they did wrong and request help fixing the problem.

Normalizing mistakes is particularly critical in the start-up world, where continuous learning and iteration is sacred, and "fail fast" is something of a mantra. Alexis Haselberger, a productivity, time-management, and efficiency expert with fifteen-plus years of experience in operations and human resources in the start-up world, emphasizes the importance of being "accountable, capable, and teachable" when the inevitable mistakes happen, and asking for help along the way is an integral part of the process (in the appendix you'll find the set of best practices she developed to help teams within start-ups and established companies alike foster accountability and learning).[20]

Good leaders know what they don't know, and they surround themselves with experts who can fill in the gaps. As Bill McDermott, CEO of the multibillion-dollar technology company SAP SE puts it, "Every leader has to have the humility to recognize that their success will be based on choosing the very best people."[21] When Christina Keller became president and CEO of Cascade Engineering, a global manufacturing firm that specializes in large-piece plastic injection molding, her first move was to assess her senior team, understand her own strengths and weaknesses, and then hire people who complemented her strengths and offset her weaknesses.[22] By doing so, she created an in-house network of experts that she could ask for help.

This insight highlights a second point: asking for help should be a part of *everyone's* job, from the summer intern right up to the top leadership. My literary agent Jim Levine, whose philosophy for running the agency he cofounded—the Levine Greenberg Rostan Literary Agency in New York City—is a living example of this book's message, makes help-seeking an explicit expectation by including it in the written guidelines of his agency. Items like "There is no such thing as a stupid question; you always have permission to ASK" and "You WILL make mistakes; that is one of the best ways to learn" help to create an environment where everyone working at the agency feels safe asking for help. (See the appendix for the complete list of guidelines.)

CHOOSING YOUR TOOLS

Now that you've set the stage for team success, the next step is to choose the tools that will make asking for help a routine, everyday practice in the life of the team. As I mentioned above, these decisions should be made via a discussion and consensus.

Huddles: Impromptu and Formal

When John Clendenin was hired to manage a logistics group at Xerox Corporation, the company wasn't known for being an open, collaborative culture. For example, when someone got stuck or needed help on a problem or project, the typical bureaucratic routine was to schedule a meeting; yet the challenge of coordinating calendars usually meant that person might be stuck for days waiting for the meeting to take place. John decided to change all that, implementing a practice called "impromptu huddles." Now, if a team member got stuck on a problem, needed some advice, or wanted to brainstorm, the person would call a quick huddle, rounding up people who might be able to help. The expectation was that, if asked, others would immediately stop what they were doing and huddle up.[23]

Impromptu huddles offer an opportunity to tap collective resources for new perspectives, ideas, and solutions, and are particularly effective when you need something quickly, whether it's to meet a tight deadline, to get unstuck on a problem, or to move a stalled project forward.[24] You don't have to schedule a meeting for the following week or wait for people to respond to an email. You don't have to take the time to figure out in advance whom to ask, and you can share your request with multiple people at once, rather than having to take it from person to person.

At IDEO, impromptu huddles are often used as a forum for brainstorming.[25] By definition, design involves coming up with something new and novel. A designer's job is to explore unfamiliar territory and routinely run into the unknown. Getting stuck is a normal part of the process. So, at IDEO, as soon as designers run into a problem or don't know something, they quickly gather a group of colleagues for an impromptu brainstorming session to help them get unstuck, get the information or insight they need, solve a problem, and so on.

Impromptu huddles, as the name implies, are informal sessions, called as needed. But huddles also can be formal, regularly scheduled meetings that follow a script or set agenda. For example, department leaders at one large manufacturing company have implemented a daily leadership huddle that always covers safety, recognition, urgent issues, as well as an open round table in which people make and grant requests. At Zingerman's Community of Businesses, the network of Ann Arbor–based businesses I mentioned earlier, the huddle is an integral part of organizational culture. Zingerman's has 45+ teams that hold voluntary huddles regularly, most of them on a weekly basis. A typical huddle is less than an hour, and follows a regular agenda, which includes a quick icebreaker, a discussion of the week's customer feedback (good and bad), a line-item review of financial and operational results, the troubleshooting of problems and delegation of new tasks, and finally, announcements and appreciations. Consistent with the company's values—e.g., everyone participates in running the business—the huddle leader is always an employee, rather than the business managing partner. Huddles create a psychologically safe place to ask for help—and as a result, they improve productivity, problem solving, and both individual and organizational learning.

Stand-up

The stand-up is a widespread practice in information technology and software development companies that has enormous potential for use in many other settings. Stand-ups occur on a regular schedule—generally at the same time every day of the work week—but take less time than formal huddles.

In a typical stand-up, everyone stands in a circle and takes turns giving a brief update (if some team members work in a different location, they will generally video-conference into the meeting). At the software firm Atlassian, each team member answers three questions: "What did I work on yesterday? What am I working on today? What issues are blocking me?"[26] Menlo Innovations follows a similar pattern, but adds a more powerful question: What help do I need? Including this question as part of the ritual makes people feel more comfortable asking for help because it establishes asking as normal and expected behavior.

A typical stand-up is usually limited to fifteen minutes to encourage efficient communication and ensure the meeting doesn't take up too much of the workday. Of course, the duration and frequency of stand-ups vary according to the needs of the group; what matters is having a regular schedule so that the stand-up becomes a normal and expected part of the work routine.

People tend to associate the stand-up meeting with small, scrappy technology start-ups, but the stand-up model is actually useful in so many other types of organizations beyond the world of IT and software development. For example, staff at the Center for Positive Organizations (CPO) have a daily stand-up whose purpose, says Managing Director Chris White, "is to facilitate the sharing of information, and asking for and receiving help. As a happy by-product, it also fosters supportive relationships between team members."[27] In a novel twist, the stand-up is facilitated by the newest person to join the team. As Chris explains it, this is a message about their team values: that anyone can lead. And it's a way of emphasizing how they "seek to provide facilitation and leadership opportunities to more than the most senior people on the team."

By the same token, stand-ups can be done on a much larger scale. For example, at Nationwide Insurance, a Fortune 100 company with $46 billion in annual sales, each of the nearly three hundred teams within the software development and operations group conducts regular stand-up meetings. During my visit to Nationwide's headquarters in Columbus, Ohio, IT executive Tom Paider and I walked the floors to see the system in action. Every team holds its stand-up in front of a physical whiteboard displaying the team's workflow. This allows everyone to see at a glance what is being done, what needs to be done, who is doing what, where help is needed, where people are stuck, and so on.

Nationwide utilizes a four-tier management system, with stand-ups conducted at each level. The work done at each level is different, but the objectives are the same: accountability, collaboration, process improvement, and problem solving.[28] It works something like this: frontline employees (Tier I) have stand-ups every day to discuss workflow, the previous day's work, and the current day's work. Any issue or problem that can't be solved is escalated to the next level. Frontline managers (Tier II) also have daily stand-ups, where they review metrics from frontline activities and address problems or requests that escalated from Tier 1, usually by providing coaching and feedback to frontline employees. Here, too, any issues that can't be resolved are escalated to the executive team (Tier III), who provide coaching and feedback to Tier II. Finally, Tier IV—the c-suite—meets weekly to review big-picture strategy, trends, and continuous improvement opportunities, as well as to deal with those obstinate problems that the previous tiers weren't able to resolve. The brilliance of this four-tier system, in other words, is that it's a built-in mechanism for lower-tier teams to request help from higher-tier ones.

Reciprocity Ring

The Reciprocity Ring is a guided activity that makes it easy for people to tap into the giving power of a network to obtain the resources they need. (I am a cofounder, board member, and a shareholder in Give and Take, Inc., which owns the Reciprocity Ring and the digital platform Givitas.) Over 100,000 people in companies and universities around the world have used this tool; I've personally used it at places like Google, Consumers Energy, General Motors, Morton Salt, and Blue Cross Blue Shield. Adam Grant has used it at IBM, Citigroup, Estée Lauder, UPS, and others.[29]

The activity is done in a group of twenty to twenty-four people, but there is no limit to the number of groups. The largest Reciprocity Ring event to date occurred at Harvard Business School, where they conducted forty simultaneous Reciprocity Rings for more than nine hundred MBAs!

With a little bit of training, anyone can facilitate a Reciprocity Ring.* The process is simple but has to be done in a particular sequence of steps. Generally, it works this way. Taking turns, each participant announces a request to the group. Other members of the group pause to consider how they could help: Do I have the resource the person needs? If not, do I know someone in my network who might be able to help? Because it's much easier for people to make a request when they know that everyone must make one, every participant is required to make a request; asking is the "ticket of admission" to the Reciprocity Ring. When time permits, I advocate two rounds of requesting: a round of personal requests and a round of work-related requests. The personal request round opens people up; sharing personal details about one's life humanizes the workplace, improving the group's communication, collaboration, and performance.[30] Getting help on a personal matter fosters gratitude, builds high-quality connections, and promotes future cooperation on both personal matters and requests related to work.

Sometimes Adam conducts an informal variation of the Reciprocity Ring in his classes at Wharton; once it was

---

* If you are interested in learning how to use or facilitate the Reciprocity Ring, contact Give and Take, Inc. at giveandtakeinc.com.

even featured on an episode of *Good Morning America*.[31] He calls it the Five-Minute Favor. While it is not as powerful as the Reciprocity Ring tool itself, this activity is one way to get started. Here's how this informal variation works. Each participant gets one piece of flip-chart paper and writes a request on the top half, leaving the bottom half blank, then sticks the page on the wall of the room. Everyone walks around the room, reading each request, and writing their names underneath any they believe they can help with. Adam once signed his name to the request one student made to spend time with famous chef-restaurateur David Chang. Turned out that Adam had the chef on his cellphone contact list and made the connection right then and there.

When I conduct the Reciprocity Ring, I emphasize that requests can be for literally anything, as long as they follow the SMART criteria I described in Chapter 4 (that is, specific, meaningful, action-oriented, realistic, and within a specified time-frame). SMART requests can be for something as small as a restaurant recommendation, or so big and bold that it may literally change someone's life—as was the case for Cristina, whose miraculous story you read in Chapter 1. Participants are often hesitant to make a request so large that it seems unlikely or impossible to fulfill. But having conducted the Reciprocity Ring many hundreds of times, I have witnessed many stories of requests that seemed impossible but were in fact fulfilled. For example, in one Reciprocity Ring, a participant I'll call Mark (not his real name) disclosed that he was adopted at birth and yearned to know his biological parents' last name. Even Mark clearly thought this was a long shot, but then someone in the group spoke up. It turned out that he was also adopted and had discovered his biological parents' last name through a combination of DNA genealogy and information he requested from the government under the Freedom of Information Act (FOIA). He happily shared his knowledge with Mark and even coached him through the process. In the end, Mark got the information he was after—as well as a valuable reminder that you truly can never know what's possible until you ask.

Work- or business-related requests are not always quite so dramatic, but they are quite often essential for solving problems, getting critical resources, and improving individual and team performance. For example, in one session, an engineer in a large engineering consulting company requested recommendations for firms with 3D modeling capabilities for a proposed multilevel rental car facility, while another engineer asked for high-quality online technical training relevant to the large-scale projects the company designs and builds. Both received the help they needed. At a leading South American manufacturer of automotive components, an executive announced in the Reciprocity Ring that he had to deliver a highly technical presentation to a potential new client and asked for good examples of similar presentations so that he could learn from them. He immediately got four offers of help.

The return on investment (ROI) in the Reciprocity Ring is impressive. When we conduct the Reciprocity Ring with only twenty-four participants and in just two and a half hours, we've calculated that the ideas, solutions, and referrals generated in the activity yield cost savings and revenue generation of anywhere from $150,000 to $400,000, as well as time savings to the tune of 1,600 hours or more. In some cases, the dollar value is much higher. At the

South American manufacturer I mentioned above, the total value of the Reciprocity Ring was greater than ten million dollars. And when large groups use the Reciprocity Ring, the benefits multiply.

The power of the Reciprocity Ring is how it taps the deep well of hidden resources and networks that exist in every group. And much like a muscle, the more the Reciprocity Ring is used, the more powerful it becomes. That's because when the activity is repeated over time, people have learned to expect positive responses, which gives them the confidence to make bigger and bigger requests. The returns to the team and each individual member on it grow exponentially in what is truly a virtuous cycle.

Troikas and Wise Crowds

In my MBA classroom, workshops, and keynote speeches, I often use two practices that focus explicitly on asking for and giving help: "Troika Consulting" and "Wise Crowds."[32] Troika Consulting is a creative thirty-minute activity that unlocks the flow of help and advice among teammates or colleagues. The team splits into groups of three (hence the name) and each member of a troika takes a turn playing the role of "the client," who has one or two minutes to describe a challenge or project and ask for help. The other two are "consultants," who have one to two minutes to ask clarifying questions, then several minutes to provide ideas, information, referrals, advice, and so on, just as they would in a real consulting session. This sequence is repeated two more times, so that each member of a troika gets to be the client and have his or her problems solved, or requests granted.

The structure of Wise Crowds is the same as Troika Consulting, but each group is larger (four or five people) and more time is spent on each step. As with any such exercise, diverse teams or groups are helpful, because you draw on a variety of perspectives, experiences, knowledge, and networks.

Plug-and-Play Requesting Routines

Huddles, stand-ups, Reciprocity Rings, Troikas, and Wise Crowds all work because they normalize the process of making requests—the crux of the giving-receiving cycle—while also bringing out the natural helpfulness in us all. What's unique about plug-and-play routines is that, unlike the aforementioned practices that require setting aside time in your workweek, they can be embedded in existing schedules, meetings, workshops, or events.

Consider, for example, a plug-and-play requesting routine used at DoSomething.org, a digital platform that has mobilized 5.5 million young people across the United States and 131 countries to engage offline in causes, social change initiatives, and civic actions.[33] Every Wednesday, DoSomething employees gather at 2:30 P.M. in the office "pit" for a weekly staff meeting. Part of the regular agenda is to invite each person to either celebrate an accomplishment of the past week, describe a goal for the upcoming one, or make a request for advice or assistance.[34] Other staff members can respond on the spot, or after the meeting. And they do.

Even one-on-one meetings are opportunities for plug-and-play. When the Detroit-based utility company DTE Energy found itself struggling to weather the financial crisis of 2008, Executive Vice President Ron May held regular one-on-one meetings with his direct reports, directors, and vice presidents.[35] Each fifteen-minute meeting was a conversation guided by questions like: What problem are you working on? What is the desired target condition (future state)? What obstacles stand in your way?

Over time, people felt psychologically safe enough not only to reveal what their obstacles were, but also to ask for what they needed to remove them. For example, Ron explains, a person working on a process change might ask for permission to go outside of procedure; or a person stuck on some facet of a big project might ask for time away to devote to a specific problem. Ultimately, this approach led to greater improvements and savings, as well as stronger relationships. DTE Energy did many other things that helped them through the financial crisis, but the application of this discipline played a key role in their recovery process.

Plug-and-play can be embedded in meetings of any kind: staff meetings, progress update meetings, performance reviews, feedback sessions, planning meetings, community of practice meetings, employee resource group meetings, training sessions, and even in informal lunch meetings. Look at your calendar for the next two weeks. Where can you experiment with a plug-and-play requesting routine?

One-Problem-a-Week Whiteboard

Two heads are better than one, especially when solving complex engineering problems. When Kevin Blue was working at pharmaceutical giant Pfizer, he and five other industrial engineers came up with an idea that grew into a routine way of asking for help.

Every Monday, the engineers would pose one technical problem in the weekly staff meeting. They would write it out on the whiteboard in the entryway of the department so that everyone on the team could work on the problem, but it would not be discussed until Friday afternoon. "This would give everyone five days to solve the problem or challenge the solution," Kevin explains. The exercise was so effective at producing solutions to the team's most vexing problems that the practice soon spread to all engineering disciplines at Pfizer.[36]

There are many, many variations of the One-Problem-a-Week Whiteboard. At one large company I know, for example, people post ad-hoc requests on a flip chart and teammates read and respond to them when they can. What variation can you experiment with?

SUMMARY

High-performing teams are psychologically safe places in which team members are enabled to ask for and give help. Building an effective team begins with setting the stage for success by selecting people for the team who are inclined to be giver-requesters, and by establishing norms that foster psychological safety and support the cycle of giving and receiving. Team leaders should reinforce these norms by regularly asking for help themselves (as well as giving it), and by making asking a part of everyone's job description. Teams can choose from the toolbox offered in this chapter—impromptu huddles, formal huddles, stand-ups, Reciprocity Rings, Troikas and Wise Crowds, plug-and-play requesting routines, and One-Problem-a-Week Whiteboards—and adapt them as needed to their individual goals or project.

REFLECTIONS AND ACTIONS

1. Is your workplace psychologically safe for people to ask for what they need? Why or why not? (Take the assessment below to quantify your perceptions.)
2. Do new teams rush to get started with work, or do they take time to set the stage for success?
3. Do you hire people who are inclined to be giver-requesters?
4. Do your team norms validate, support, and promote asking?
5. Are you a role model of asking behavior?
6. What team tools do you already use? How well do they work?
7. Have your team pick a new team tool and try it for at least thirty days. Tweak and customize as necessary to fit your situation.
8. Look for opportunities to insert requesting routines in your daily interactions and meetings. You can even look for these opportunities in your personal life!
9. If you are assembling a new team, follow the prescriptions in this chapter for building a successful team.

APPENDIX

Handling Mistakes Best Practices

Alexis Haselberger

We all make mistakes once in a while. But what sets us apart is how we handle mistakes once they happen. Accountability is a central tenet of success at work (and in life), and how you handle yourself when you do something wrong can make all the difference in how you are perceived going forward.

So, here's how to ensure that you come across as accountable, capable, and teachable when you do make a mistake.

Take Responsibility

- As soon as you realize you've made a mistake, own up to it. This is hard, and it will feel bad. But we should feel bad when we make a mistake, because it's that negative feeling that helps give us the motivation to avoid mistakes in the future.
- The sooner you own up to the mistake, the sooner it can be fixed and the less likely it will be to have a cascading negative effect.
- Avoid blame. If you made the mistake, you made it. Sure, there could be contributing factors, but you can only control yourself and you are responsible for any mistakes you make.

1. Take Action

- Reflect: Now that you've found the mistake, think about why it happened. See if you can figure out what led to it. Was it a simple oversight caused by not paying attention? Did you receive the wrong info from someone else? Were the instructions confusing?
- Resolve: Fix the mistake. Whatever happened will need to be fixed, whether it's a client issue, for data integrity reasons, etc. If you aren't sure how to fix the mistake, seek help.
- Move forward: Now that the mistake is fixed, it's time for a postmortem. You don't want to make the same mistake twice, so figure out what steps you need to take to ensure that the conditions that led to it are not repeated, and that this mistake won't happen again.

2. Respond/Resolve

- When resolving and responding to a mistake, there are four key elements that must be addressed: What happened? How did it happen? How did we fix it? What are we doing to make sure that it won't happen again?
- You'll want to ensure that you follow this structure in responding to whomever was affected by your mistake, and your manager, if necessary.

Jim Levine's Assistant Guidelines

Levine Greenberg Rostan Literary Agency

1. We hired you because of your talent and potential, not because we expect you to know everything.
2. There is no such thing as a stupid question; you always have permission to ASK.
3. You WILL make mistakes; that is one of the best ways to learn.
4. The rule of thumb for anybody starting a new job is that it takes six months to begin feeling comfortable with what you are doing.
5. Our agency's reputation is our single most valuable asset. You are the first person that many clients, potential clients, and publishers will deal with when they contact our agency. The way you deal with EVERYBODY has an impact on our reputation.
6. I will always look like I'm busy—that's just my manner. Don't let that put you off from interrupting whatever I'm doing. Just signal me that you need my attention.
7. As you learn the way we do things, you may question why we do them that way. Don't be afraid to ask "why" or to suggest alternate ways of doing things. We are always looking for ways to improve what we are doing and how we are doing it.
8. If you ever feel that things aren't working the way you'd like in your job—even small things—let me know. We like to address problems, and hopefully solve them, as soon as they come up. The worst thing to do is let small issues fester into big ones. (We tell our clients exactly the same thing.)

9. We value initiative. Make your opinions and suggestions known—about submission letters, proposals, anything. And pitch in with ideas for new projects: topics we should find a writer for or people we should go after as clients.

10. While you are reporting directly to me, you are working for the whole team, and everybody on the team will value the same sort of feedback that I am asking of you.

Measuring Team Psychological Safety

To what extent do you agree or disagree with each statement? Circle one response for each.	Strongly Disagree	Disagree	Disagree Somewhat	Neither Agree nor Disagree	Agree Somewhat	Agree	Strongly Agree
1. If you make a mistake on this team, it is often held against you.	1	2	3	4	5	6	7
2. Members of this team are able to bring up problems and tough issues.	1	2	3	4	5	6	7
3. People on this team sometimes reject others for being different.	1	2	3	4	5	6	7
4. It is safe to take a risk on this team.	1	2	3	4	5	6	7

To what extent do you agree or disagree with each statement? Circle one response for each.	Strongly Disagree	Disagree	Disagree Somewhat	Neither Agree nor Disagree	Agree Somewhat	Agree	Strongly Agree
5. It is difficult to ask other members of this team for help.	1	2	3	4	5	6	7
6. No one on this team would deliberately act in a way that undermines my efforts.	1	2	3	4	5	6	7
7. Working with members of this team, my unique skills and talents are valued and utilized.	1	2	3	4	5	6	7

Source: Edmondson, A. C. "Psychological Safety and Learning Behavior in Work Teams." *Administrative Science Quarterly* 44:350–83 (1999).

Scoring: Questions 1, 3, and 5 are worded in the negative so they have to be reverse coded. So, for example, if you answered 7 for Question 1, change your answer to 1; if you answered 6 for Question 1, change it to 2; if you answered 5, change it to 3; if you answered 4, keep it that way; change 3 to 5, 2 to 6, and 1 to 7. Do the same reverse coding for Questions 3 and 5.

Now, add up your choices for the seven questions, and then divide the total by 7 to get the average. (If your trusted teammates also completed the quiz, average all your averages.) An average score of 6 to 7 indicates that team psychological safety is very high; an average of 1 to 2 indicates that psychological safety is very low.

Comparisons: The average team score was 5.25 in Edmondson's original study of 427 employees in 53 teams at a manufacturing firm. In a study of neonatal intensive care units that she conducted with Ingrid Nembhard, the average team score was 5.31, for 1,440 employees working in 23 teams.[37]

CHAPTER 6

ASKING ACROSS BOUNDARIES

The executives and superintendents at Kent Power, Inc. weren't listening. The superintendents, who oversaw operations, were complaining that company executives never paid attention to what they had to say, and didn't communicate out into the field to keep everyone in the know. Meanwhile, the executives were pointing fingers at the superintendents, saying that they didn't even bother to read the memos the executives sent out.

Kent Power builds and maintains power lines, electrical substations, cellular towers, and telecommunications infrastructure. Communication across the hierarchy is critical in this specialized industry, but the executives and superintendents just weren't hearing one another, and the business was suffering as a result.

The executives knew they needed help and asked for it, bringing in a veteran business coach, Dave Scholten, to help them get things on track.[1] Dave proposed designing a mini-game (a tool I will tell you more about later in Chapter 7) to improve communication across the executive-superintendent boundary. They called it "Can you hear me now?" after the well-known Verizon tagline.

The mini-game ran for three months. In the first month, the seventeen executives and superintendents would have regular one-on-one phone calls; each call had to be at least ten minutes long, and each person had to initiate sixteen phone calls—one to every person in the group—during the month. The key rule, however, had to do with the topic of conversation: they could *not* talk about work. All other topics—hobbies, current events, books and movies, football, the weather—were on the table. Just not work. Dave required each person to jot down notes about the call on the company's shared drive—including at least two insights from the conversation. These records were visible to all, so that everyone could learn from and about one another.

In the second month, everyone had to initiate *two* phone calls with each person. In the third month, the number of calls doubled again—*four* phone calls per person. These numbers add up quickly. All told, the executives and superintendents spent hundreds of hours on the phone with one another. All in ninety days. And never talking about work.

As you can imagine, the "no work conversations" rule led to a lot of grumbling and consternation. What would they talk about if they couldn't talk about work? After all, work was the only context they shared, the single thing they knew they already had in common. And that was exactly the point. With this default conversational topic off-limits, they were forced to learn about each other's lives *outside* the four walls of the office. It felt strange, at first, to ask and answer questions like "How did you meet your spouse or partner?" but over time it got progressively easier, to the point where their calls with each colleague became more like one extended conversation full of new inquiries and thoughtful follow-up questions. They talked about family, friends, hardships, triumphs, and dreams; they connected on a personal and emotional level.

Once the three months were over, the seventeen leaders of Kent Power could finally hear one another. "The end result of the game," says Dave Scholten, "was the breaking down of silos, and getting them to understand each other."[2] In fact, "Can you hear me now?" was such a success, Kent Power decided to turn the mini-game tool from a onetime intervention into a regular practice across the business. (See Chapter 7 for mini-game guidelines.)

Silos are problems for most organizations. Some take the form of a barrier between levels of the hierarchy, like at Kent Power. Others are divides between departments, business units, teams, or physical locations. For some companies, silos stand between an organization and its customers and suppliers. Asking and collaborating across such boundaries can reap measurable benefits for individuals, such as improved access to knowledge, ideas, opportunities, and other resources, which in turn elevate productivity and performance; for companies, bridging boundaries yields higher revenues and profits, more innovation, stronger client and customer loyalty, and even greater ability to attract and retain talent.[3]

Asking across boundaries opens up a world of resources. Sometimes, the resource you need is close by, right in your team, department, office, or local community, and all you have to do is ask for it. Other times, however, what you need is out there, somewhere in the world, but you don't know where. You have to ask across boundaries to find it.

In our personal lives, too, we often unwittingly erect boundaries that close ourselves off to a giant body of resources. For example, many of us draw a hard line between "life" and "work." We assume that personal requests have no place in a work setting, and by the same token that we shouldn't trouble our friends and family with requests having to do with our jobs. But this couldn't be further from the case.

When Jim Mallozzi took over as CEO and chairman of the board of Prudential Real Estate and Relocation, the company was in trouble. Clients were unhappy, talent was jumping ship, and the business was hemorrhaging millions of dollars. Jim was determined to do whatever it took to get the company back on track. There was just one problem: Jim's home was in Connecticut, but he was spending most of his time at Prudential Real Estate's major U.S. offices in California, Arizona, and New Jersey. Jim hated being away from home so much; he missed his family, and his wife and daughters missed him. Worse yet, the high demands of his job had started to take a toll on his health; he was stressed, and because he was constantly either working or on the road, he wasn't exercising and had gained weight.[4]

Jim knew that if he wanted things to change, he was going to need some help. But with his family so far away, he also knew that he would need to find a source of more day-to-day support. Then, at a town hall with all his associates, he got his chance. After laying out the company's plans and business goals for the year, as previous CEOs always had done, he tried something unconventional: he announced his three personal goals as well. "Stay happily married to my wife of some thirty years, don't miss any important dates/events for my two daughters back home, lose twenty pounds and eat better." Then he asked everyone in the audience to help.

And that they did. One associate offered to be Jim's running partner; another wouldn't let him eat dessert at the end of team dinners. Many associates, Jim said, would stop by when he was having lunch in the company cafeteria to make sure he was eating a salad.

Jim was a role model of taking permission to ask, in a manner similar to Dr. Salort-Pons, the director of the Detroit Institute of Arts you read about in Chapter 5. Only Jim did it on a much bigger stage, urging the thousands of associates in the town hall to follow suit. Pretty soon, they were all sharing both their professional *and* personal goals and supporting one another in their efforts to achieve them. "It's fun, helpful, and very insightful to see what folks want to accomplish," Jim says. "I think of it as New Year's resolutions on steroids!"

Jim's approach to goals as requests initiated a company culture of giving and receiving. And not only that; much like the "Can you hear me now?" exercise at Kent Power, this practice also forged stronger connections up and down and across the organization, which in turn sparked new ideas, novel business strategies, and boosted communication and the circulation of resources throughout the company. "With everyone's help, not only did we achieve our business turnaround," Jim concludes, "but I am still happily married, I didn't miss any important events for my daughters, and I lost twenty-five pounds!"

By setting goals and making them public, you give yourself additional incentive to reach them. And by reaching across silos and asking for help, you greatly increase your chances of doing just that. Sometimes the people you least expect can become your support group, providing encouragement and holding you accountable—as you do the same for them.

THE DIVERSITY BONUS

Think about the last time you flew out of your local airport. Did you wait at the gate, unable to board, for what seemed like an eternity—even as you can see your plane outside, just sitting there? This frustrating delay is a function of what's called "turnaround"—the time it takes to unload a plane and get it ready for your flight. The typical turnaround time is forty-five to sixty minutes. But Southwest Airlines figured out how to cut turnaround time to a mere ten minutes.[5]

All airlines are motivated to reduce turnaround time, not just because it makes passengers happy, but because they don't make money when aircraft sit on the tarmac. But executing a turnaround isn't as simple as you might think; it involves a series of diverse tasks that must be completed successfully under severe time pressure, such as deplaning passengers and baggage, unloading cargo and mail, refueling, cleaning and restocking the plane, conducting safety checks, and then onboarding a new flight crew, passengers, baggage, and cargo. So, how did

Southwest figure out how to get all this done in a fraction of the time it takes their competitors?

The conventional approach to solving this problem would have been to engage a team of operations and logistics experts and have them figure it out. We tend to look to experts because of their deep knowledge of a subject. The problem is that the very depth of their knowledge is exactly what introduces unconscious bias into problem solving, argues complexity theorist and diversity expert Scott Page.[6] Complex problems, Scott says, require "cognitive diversity"—different ways of thinking, varied perspectives, dissimilar worldviews—much more than expertise. Put the right mix of diverse people on a complex problem, his research shows, and you get what Scott calls a "diversity bonus"—a leap in performance and results.[7] Southwest assembled a diverse team of pilots, baggage handlers, flight attendants, ground crew, airport workers, and regulators to work on the problem, and that is the chief reason why it was able to figure out how to achieve the fastest turnaround time in the industry.

The tools in this section will show how you can reap a similar "diversity bonus" by broadening the pool of people—and resources—you can tap into with your requests.

ORGANIZATIONAL PRACTICES THAT ASK ACROSS BOUNDARIES

In 2016, I gave a TEDx talk at the Power Center for the Performing Arts in Ann Arbor, Michigan. The topic of my talk was the theme of this book: Asking drives the giving-receiving cycle. I wanted the audience to *experience* the power of asking, not just hear about it. So, at the end of my formal presentation, my two assistants and I quickly divided the audience of 1,350 into small groups and asked them to engage in a rapid-fire round-robin of asking for and giving help. After twenty minutes or so, we asked everyone who had received help to stand. Applause erupted when people looked around and saw how many people were on their feet. You could feel the energy in the room. We estimated, conservatively, that 70 percent of the 1,350 participants received something they needed, personally or professionally. This story highlights how having the right organizational practices in place can help us maximize the benefits of asking across boundaries.

Cross-Collaboration Workshops

What do NASCAR, Le Mans, drag racing, and Bonneville Salt Flats land-speed events have in common? General Motors races in them all. But these events aren't just fun and games for the automaker. Rather, they are opportunities for engineers to try out new technologies and test vehicles under strenuous conditions. The result is more reliable and safer cars on our roads and highways. But getting it right requires a high degree of collaboration and coordination between engineers, technicians, designers, and drivers: something that is almost impossible to achieve when people work in silos.

That was the situation Prabjot Nanua faced as GM's global director of two separate divisions within the organization: Advanced Engine Engineering and Racing Engineering. It might seem as though these two areas would have many similar functions, but they operated with such dramatically different time horizons and schedules that ongoing collaboration was difficult. Advanced Engineering works on coming up with new innovations that will boost engine performance and lower costs. Their work may not see production for years to come. Racing Engineering, on the other hand, focuses on making small fixes and improvements to existing engines from one weekly race to the next. For them, getting their work done before the next race is everything.

By the time Prabjot took the helm of the two programs, some ideas generated by the Advanced Engineering team had been implemented in the racing program, but he saw the potential for much more. To increase give-and-take across silos, Prabjot conceived of the idea of cross-collaboration workshops that brought engineers from both teams together to talk about the goals, technologies, and challenges that each group faced.[8] Prabjot didn't dictate what would be discussed; rather, he had the engineers rate their interest in various topics, and focused subsequent workshops on those with the most votes.

Soon, the monthly workshops became invaluable forums for the engineers to ask questions, make requests, and offer suggestions and advice. For example, on the rare occasions when the Advanced Engineering team would need some part to be delivered quickly in order to keep their project on schedule, they could reach out to someone on the Racing team and ask how "they can leverage the processes developed by the Racing team to acquire parts and services quickly," says Prabjot.[9]

The new-partner introduction forum at Zingerman's Community of Business is a ritual that not only crosses organizational boundaries, but it also reaches outside the confines of the organization to solicit the support of the broader community as well. This all-morning event occurs anytime someone has been elevated to managing partner status. All managing partners from Zingerman's ten semi-autonomous businesses are invited, as well as interested employees, friends, and visitors (I participated in one where I counted sixty people in attendance). Everyone—including visitors—is asked to announce what they will do or contribute to help the new partner be successful. For example, the chief accountant might pledge to always deliver accurate financial statements on time, and to be available for consultations on the numbers. A recently retired partner might volunteer to help out with whatever task the new partner might have. A few tech-savvy employees might offer to help spread the word about the new business on social media. These are examples I've actually witnessed, and they highlight what a diverse set of resources you get access to when you reach across boundaries to ask for help.

Continuing Education Programs

I've taught in many executive education programs over the years. One trend I've seen is the rise of customized programs designed for corporate clients. Unlike open enrollment programs, where anyone can sign up, a custom program is open only to employees of a given company and is tailored to that company's specific business objectives, priorities, and needs. For example, many executives at General Motors have participated in a program called "Transformational Leadership," a partnership with Stanford University.[10] Each cohort consists of a thoughtfully designed and diverse set of thirty-five to forty executives from around the globe. These executives participate in five sessions over the course of a year, with each one held in a different country. "Perhaps the most significant part of this program," writes former GM Chief Talent Officer Michael Arena in *Adaptive Space,* ". . . is the social capital that is created."[11]

What does it mean—specifically—to say that social capital is created? Social capital simply refers to your network and the resources it contains. Through the GM program, executives build social capital by meeting people from different business units and countries, getting to know one another, working together on team projects, and socializing. Through these experiences, they forge new bonds—and access to new resources—that persist after the program is over.

This was certainly the case for Robert, a national sales manager for a major corporation, when he heard about a problem from an irate store manager.[12] His company sold its products through company-owned retail stores, and apparently someone in headquarters had sent a letter to customers that inadvertently directed them to the wrong stores. When Robert looked into it, he discovered that the letter had originated in the department of someone he met in his executive education program. He called this person and together they resolved the matter quickly and effectively. Since then, Robert told me, he has resolved several other problems by connecting with various participants in the program—in other words, by tapping his new social capital.

How does one facilitate the creation of social capital in an executive education program? We don't leave it to chance. Right from day one, we assign seating so that everyone is sitting in groups of six people from different units and countries. Then we rotate assigned seating every day after. We group new people together when we have teams participate in an in-class design project, and then mix those groups up again when we send them out of the classroom to interview consumers, ideate, and build prototypes. And we provide educational experiences in the evenings, where participants can socialize. It's hard to leave the program *without* having created new personal bonds across all kinds of social, organizational, and geographic boundaries.

A custom executive education program may not be in the cards for you right now, but there are other practices that mimic them. For example, many companies have job rotation programs for new hires and for current employees, such as the IT company ManTech, the NFL, Deloitte, and Abbott Laboratories, among many others.[13] In each of these programs, an employee is rotated from unit to unit (or from one location to another), spending several weeks, months, or even a year or more in each one. This kind of job rotation is most common for new hires, but it is also used for current employees as a way of enriching the work experience, promoting learning, and building new social capital across silos, which they can access when they have a request. And it's also a powerful learning mechanism for the employer, in that it provides information about people's interests and skill sets that helps them find the best matches of people and jobs.[14]

Flexible Budgeting

Most managers hold their budgets tighter than bark on a tree. The idea of giving a portion of a department's budget—even when it has surplus funds—to another department or project is unthinkable. But that's what happens regularly at Hopelab, a social innovation lab in San Francisco, California, that designs science-based technologies aimed at improving the health and well-being of teens and young adults. Once, for example, a vice president brought forward an exciting strategic communications opportunity that COO Dan Cawley believed "could highlight to a large targeted audience our efforts in childhood obesity as well as discuss how we meld behavioral science, design and technology to develop our products that make kids healthy." It was a great opportunity, with only one snag—the $100,000 price tag had not been budgeted. Being a nonprofit, Hopelab operates with a tight budget, but even so, their practice of flexible budgeting allowed them to easily pull together the funds.[15]

Of course, not every budget manager was able to free up funds and still hit their departmental goals and milestones. But one project manager said that he could contribute a large five-figure sum if his group scaled back one of their efforts, which still left him enough resources to keep the project going. This large sum, plus smaller amounts from nearly all departments, allowed them to reach the $100,000 goal.

The practice of flexible budgeting not only enables Hopelab to respond to emerging challenges and opportunities in ways that a traditional approach to budgeting would not be able to accommodate, it also builds transparency and trust and fosters collaboration across organizational divides. And, Dan notes, the process is "unemotional"—contrary to what one might think, it doesn't give rise to turf wars or drama. In fact, "People are completely generous," he says. "The budget funds flow and ebb easily between projects."

And this generous approach to budgeting doesn't work only for a nonprofit like Hopelab. It also worked at Prudential Real Estate and Relocation, though it went by a different name: Stone Soup budgeting, after the ancient folktale that illustrates the value of sharing and cooperation.

Typically, corporate budgets are based on past budgets (what we need this budget year is based on what we spent last year), and often devolve into a battle between division leaders vying for discretionary dollars. The CEO often plays "King Solomon," says Prudential Real Estate CEO Jim Mallozzi, "underfunding projects to the point where neither is successful, or even worse, a great idea not going ahead."[16] Which is why Jim tried a different method for annual budgeting and as-needed during the budget year. First, he convened a large group of senior and middle-level executives to evaluate new ideas and projects to ensure consistency with the company's core philosophy and mission. Then each department head or manager would commit to contribute something to making the project a success. Some contributed budget dollars, others offered expertise or project management resources. And some contributed in the form of public acknowledgment and support, which communicated throughout the organization that the project was important. "I knew we were succeeding," Jim recalls, "when—during very tough discussions—groups and leaders would willingly give up both budget dollars and their best people to tackle a particular challenge."

Stone Soup budgeting shifted leaders from the typical us-versus-them orientation to a we're-all-in-this-together orientation. Success became all about the collective win rather than the individual ones. As Jim put it, "Applying the principles of Stone Soup—if you want to eat well you must positively contribute—allowed us to become truly vested in enterprise initiatives."

Brain Trusts

There will, however, be times when asking across silos within your company is either impractical or simply doesn't cast the net widely enough. "If you run an organization, there are a bunch of things you can't talk about with your spouse or your employees," says Rich Smalling, CEO of American Innovations, a provider of products and services to manage and protect the nation's oil and gas pipeline infrastructure.[17] In cases like these, you will need to look outside of your organization (and your family) to get expert input and advice.

For this, what you need is a brain trust.

Rich's brain trust is called "YPO," formerly known as Young Presidents' Organization. YPO was founded in 1950 in New York City; today, it's a global network of more than 27,000 chief executives in over 130 countries.[18] Forums— local groups of eight to ten peer leaders who meet monthly for two to four hours—are the heart of YPO. "Everything said is in complete and total confidence," says Rich. "We're always asking for help in the forum. You can ask for help on *anything*."

YPO chapters are the next level up, with more than 450 worldwide. Chapters are more formalized than forums, with a set calendar of monthly events, themes, speakers, and so on. Joining a chapter gives you access to a wider range of peers. And conversations are what Rich calls "forum-confidential," meaning that your ask is treated with complete confidence and trust. YPO also offers access to worldwide digital communities organized around specific topics or themes, and a private networking site called "M2Mx," where members can submit requests about any personal or business issue.

YPO is a global organization, but there are many local and regional brain trusts you can join as well. For example, BreakThrough Forums in the Chicagoland area organizes groups that bring together business leaders with shared interests and from similar-size companies. "These groups are the essence of collaboration, where c-level leaders ask for help from their peers," says Tom Caprel, who heads the organization.[19] "The members respond in a safe and nonjudgmental environment, using their own experiences as a guide for the requester."

For those who don't want to join a preexisting brain trust, it's easy to create your own. In my role as the faculty director of the Center for Positive Organizations, the members of our Executives-in-Residence program have become my informal brain trust. This august cohort of senior executives has decades of experience in corporate and civic leadership, and I can ask anything, knowing that whatever we discuss will be held in strict confidence—and that I am certain to get excellent help and advice.

USING TECHNOLOGY TO ASK ACROSS BOUNDARIES

On Wednesday, January 30, 2019, the polar vortex broke a 108-year record for the coldest January 30th in Ann Arbor, Michigan. It was -17 degrees Fahrenheit outside my home; wind chill made it feel like 40 below zero.

About ten-thirty that night, my wife and I received an emergency text from Consumers Energy, asking us to voluntarily reduce the heat in our home to 65 degrees or lower. As it turned out, there had been an equipment fire at one of Consumer Energy's natural gas compressor stations in southeast Michigan. No one was injured, but all gas flow from the station was shut off, threatening the gas supply to customers throughout the region.

I immediately dialed down my thermostat. Thousands and thousands of Michiganders did as well, and as a result gas usage dropped 10 percent systemwide. The voluntary reduction enabled Consumers Energy to provide an uninterrupted supply of gas to homes and businesses during the frigid days of the polar vortex.

This extraordinary act of collective citizenship was possible because digital technology made it easy to broadcast the ask to a huge population all at once. And these days, you don't need to have the infrastructure of a giant corporation to share a request on this kind of scale. In fact, we can all leverage the power of technology to reach broad new swaths of people and networks quickly and easily.

Random Meetups

Have you ever met an expert in the art of unarmed stage combat? I have. I work in the Ross School of Business, miles apart—physically and academically—from the School of Music, Theatre, and Dance, where students learn such skills. So, I would have been very unlikely to cross paths with an expert in unarmed stage combat had I not participated in something called "Innovate Brew."

Innovate Brew is an online system that randomly pairs faculty members from across the vast University of Michigan campus. Paired faculty meet to tell each other about their current research and other projects, and giving-receiving—either on the spot, or in the future—is an implicit part of the process. In one meetup, for example, I met an engineer who sits on a university governance committee. Later, when I had questions about policies under the committee's purview, I knew who to ask. "The idea is to get to know someone who has a completely different lens on the world," says Bill Lovejoy, creator of Innovate Brew and a professor of technology and operations at the Ross School. "You don't usually have permission to walk up and talk to strangers," Bill notes.[20] But Innovate Brew gives you permission to ask.[21]

Large-Scale Events

Not long after Jim Mallozzi took charge of Prudential Real Estate and Relocation, the company hosted a series of annual sales awards and training conventions for their many thousands of sales professionals around the world.

"The theme of my first keynote address," says Jim, "was 'change and innovation' while tapping into the 'positive power of the possible.'" At one point during his address, Jim asked the audience of 3,000 sales professionals to pull out their smartphones. Everyone groaned, assuming they were about to be instructed to turn their devices off. Instead, Jim asked them to turn their phones *on*. Then he made a request. "Text or email at least one idea about how you could help a fellow professional get a new client, improve a sale, or keep a customer for life." The text number and email address were projected on a big screen. Jim called for his smartphone onstage, using it to demonstrate what he wanted them to do.

"By the end of the conference, a mere thirty-six hours later," Jim reports, "the group had generated over 2,200 ideas!" Jim's large-scale requesting routine was so successful that it soon became a regular practice at the company.

What large-scale events does your organization host? These are ideal settings for giving and receiving on a grand scale. The old maxim is true: there *is* power in numbers. And any setting where you host or assemble large and diverse groups of people can be an opportunity to conduct a large-scale event to ask for and give help across boundaries.

Videoconferencing: Always-On or Otherwise

Like many companies, American Express is moving toward a digital workforce, whereby employees can work from almost anywhere. Luckily there is plenty of technology out there to help us stay connected across far-flung locations. Lauren Acquista, who led the digital transformation at Amex, worked in the New York office but her team was divided between New York and Palo Alto, California. So, to ensure that the flow of information and requests between the two coastal offices wouldn't suffer, each one installed a large always-on videoconferencing screen. "It felt like one team," recalls Lauren.[22] "You could just walk up to the screen and have a dialogue, ask for help, ask a question." Each screen, in other words, was like a portal to the other office.

Influence & Company, a content marketing agency headquartered in Columbia, Missouri, whose sales force works remotely, uses the software Zoom to build trust with their remote clients. "We're discussing meaningful, complicated topics when our teams are working with clients. We interview them to get personal stories that we can turn into effective online content," says Alyssa Patzius, vice president of client experience.[23] Alyssa also uses Zoom in weekly one-on-one calls with her direct reports. Seeing one another in a Zoom call, says Alyssa, makes it easier for employees to ask for what they need.

Intertek, a global inspection, product testing, and certification company, operates with a radically distributed business model, and its 43,000 employees work in a thousand labs around the globe. This distributed model allows each lab to provide tailored services to clients in its local market. And it also offers a multitude of opportunities for each of the labs to learn from one another. Each month, Scott Hanton, general manager at Intertek Allentown, Pennsylvania, hosts a Skype meeting with chemicals lab managers and staff members from labs across the United

States, with the last part of the session reserved for a "rapid-fire" session during which participants can ask questions or make requests. "People offer answers right then and there," Scott says. All kinds of information is exchanged, from tricks for working with certain instruments and chemicals, to best practices for management succession.

Rapid-fire "is about tapping into tacit knowledge, the stuff that isn't written down," Scott observes, and is particularly useful in the case of questions for which people are not finding answers in other forums. This practice is so successful that Scott has been asked to expand it next to Europe, then to Asia, and then to take it global.

Messaging Apps

When I was about to pen this section, I texted my high school son to ask for help about asking for help: "Do you use Instagram, Snapchat, or any other apps to ask for help from your friends? Could you give me a good example?"

"Yah," he texted back. "Can we talk about this when I get home?"

Later, I learned that my son uses messaging apps regularly to ask for help. One time, he used Instagram to send his friends pictures of several shirts he was thinking of buying, asking them to rate the options. More than once, he's used Snapchat to ask for details about a homework assignment he left at school. All his friends do the same.

The three most popular messaging apps in the world are WhatsApp, Facebook Messenger, and WeChat (used mostly in the Chinese market).[24] But my Weekend MBA students, who work full-time and attend classes on weekends, use GroupMe to organize group outings, ask questions about a class or assignment, share restaurant recommendations, and so on.

However, Instagram, Snapchat, WhatsApp, GroupMe, and similar social apps are generally used for personal communications; they don't comfortably cross the personal/work life divide. For that, most people opt to use enterprise social software designed specifically for the workplace—Yammer, Slack, Chatter, Jabber, Microsoft Teams, and the like.

"Slack helped to create a culture of sharing," says Lauren Acquista, whose digital accelerator team in Brooklyn, New York, uses the messaging tool to organize real-time communication by channels dedicated to specific teams, projects, interests, and more.[25] The digital accelerator has channels for both personal topics (parents, films, food, etc.) and work ones. "With technology and a younger workforce," Lauren explains, "the lines between personal and work life become blurred"—which means that employees don't hesitate to use the tool to make non-work-related requests.

The staff at Give and Take, Inc., the company I cofounded, also uses Slack, and they too have both personal and work channels. "It's great for instant messaging, project updates, and posting articles," says Sarah Allen-Short, vice president of marketing.[26] And the staff also uses it to exchange watercooler talk, happy birthdays, family photos, funny memes, book recommendations, and more.

Some companies try to discourage communication about personal matters in the workplace. This is a mistake. As we saw in the story about Kent Power, learning about our colleagues' hobbies, interests, and pastimes outside of the office builds trust, and strengthens bonds. In a study of its remote teams, Google learned that getting to know one another on a personal level is critical to team success.[27] Indeed, experts say that curiosity about colleagues' personal lives is "a key motivator for employees to engage with their company's social tools."[28] It's hard to ask for help from a relative stranger. Knowing something about others' personal lives—whether that knowledge is achieved through mini-games like "Can you hear me now?" or through social messaging apps—makes it easier.

And simply observing what people say in discussions conducted on these public messaging channels is also an effective way to learn who knows what, and who knows whom. In one rigorous study conducted in a large financial services firm, using enterprise social software for just six months led to "a 31% improvement in knowledge of who knows what and an 88% improvement in knowledge of who knows whom."[29] This knowledge helps you identify experts who can immediately answer a question or grant a request you may have or, if necessary, tell you who to ask for an introduction to another expert.

Collaborative Technology Platforms

"When and why do people ask for help at work? What do you ask for, why do you ask for it, and what motivates you to ask?" These were among the first questions I posted to the Center for Positive Organizations (CPO) Givitas community, a digital network that links all the companies and organizations in CPO's Positive Organizations Consortium. Givitas is a collaborative technology platform (CTP) I helped to design based on the principles and concepts in *All You Have to Do Is Ask;* it establishes a psychologically safe environment for requesting, giving, and receiving help across boundaries on a vast scale. In short order, I received a dozen detailed replies, providing me with fresh examples that I weaved into this book.

As I continued to research and write, I posted queries (while also responding to requests others made) to a human resource (HR) Givitas community that includes more than 1,200 HR experts from as many companies. In fact, many generous people I name in this book were ones I met for the first time after they responded to my Givitas requests. The diagram below illustrates the power of this HR giving-receiving network over just the first three months of operations (dots are people, lines are responses to requests).[30]

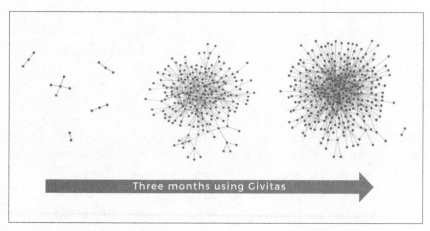

Illustration of Givitas Network Over Time, from First to Third Month

I posted requests in the *Granted* Givitas community, too, and received many useful replies. And, of course, I've offered help wherever I could.

Granted Givitas is a community we started exclusively for subscribers to Adam Grant's popular newsletter, *Granted,* where he shares insights and ideas about work and psychology. To date, over 1,300 subscribers have joined, and use it regularly to ask for and give help.

For example, one fintech start-up founder asked for introductions to like-minded folks in New York City to prevent the loneliness and isolation that can accompany the entrepreneurial lifestyle. He offered his own software and coding expertise in exchange for community support and ideation, and got five offers, ranging from potential investors to people with experience in the space who wanted to meet for coffee. When we followed up with him to see how things turned out, he valued the "pitch improvement and ongoing potential investor connections" he received at "arguably $250,000 or more if it pushes us into raising a round."

In one instance, a chief technology officer with a side interest in health was advising a start-up that focuses on fitness and strength training for vegans. He asked for advice and connections to help them get the word out about a January challenge, and received five responses with ideas the team hadn't thought of, offers to connect and brainstorm offline, and a valuable connection to the makers of a vegan documentary produced by Leonardo DiCaprio. As a result of connections made on Givitas, DiCaprio's team shared the January challenge via social media; deeper collaborations are now being explored.

Platforms like Givitas allow people to get what they need without having to repeatedly tap all the same experts or all the usual go-to people, because requests are decentralized and broadcast across the vast network.[31]

Technology-forward teams and companies can even build their own collaborative platforms from scratch. The global accounting and consulting firm PwC, for example, created Spark, a system designed and controlled by users that incorporates popular social networking features.[32] Within twelve months of launching, Spark had 100,000 active users and 95 percent of PwC staff used Spark in a ninety-day period.

The oil and gas company ConocoPhillips developed another example of a successful platform that enabled adaptable networks, agile interactions, and collaboration. At the time of this writing, more than 13,000 colleagues belonged to one or more knowledge-sharing networks, generating more than 125,000 instances of peer-to-peer problem solving and hundreds of millions of dollars of business value.[33] ConocoPhillips' CTP was guided by Dan Ranta, who was chief knowledge officer at the company for ten years. Today, he is GE's knowledge sharing leader, where, in just twenty-four months, he built 147 active business communities for a company many times the size of ConocoPhillips. The goal of each, Dan told me, is "to get the right knowledge to the right people at the right time."[34] Trust is Dan's number one concern. To that end, each community is bounded and only members can participate. And community governance is critical. All content is curated by a core team, and in addition to monitoring the performance of each platform, Dan regularly provides coaching, shares best practices, conducts internal benchmarking and many other activities to build, support, and sustain the communities. "No governance, no chance of success," Dan says.

At IBM, over 65,000 employees from around the world signed up to use Beehive, the company's global social network site, between 2007 to 2011. Much like Lauren Acquista's digital accelerator, IBM encouraged employees to use the platform to share personal details, post photos of family and fun events, and connect on a personal level.[35] In fact, researchers who analyzed Beehive found that "connecting on a social level was a source of personal satisfaction" that increased motivations to work together.[36] Beehive also uses elements of gamification to facilitate idea generation, new projects and collaborations, work-related feedback, and new connections across teams and silos. But connecting on a human level was the foundation on which these professional connections depended.

Eventually, IBM replaced Beehive with SocialBlue, eliminating Beehive's game-like features.[37] In Beehive, users earned points for posting lists, photos, and comments; they leveled up when they accumulated a certain number of points, and their badges for each new level were displayed on their user profile pages. When game features were eliminated, however, engagement on the platform dropped drastically.[38] Why? Because the removal of game features depersonalized the system, and participants lost the feeling of belonging that's vital for continued use and participation.[39]

These examples are consistent with the research showing that employees will abandon a system if they don't find enough value with it and when their peers start abandoning it.[40] "Without supportive leadership, some degree of culture change, and close alignment with other activities," says collaboration expert Heidi Gardner, a CTP won't gain traction.[41] It takes time, patience, creativity, experimentation, trial and error, learning, and relentless support to start a community, gain momentum, and get past the tipping point to a self-sustaining state. GE's Dan Ranta likens the process to the "flywheel effect" described in *Good to Great* by Jim Collins. Push and slowly the flywheel begins to turn; it gains momentum, slowly but steadily, and eventually there's a breakthrough.

SUMMARY

Asking across boundaries expands the giving-receiving network, virtually guaranteeing that you'll find the answer or resource you need. Organizational practices that bridge boundaries include cross-collaboration workshops, continuous education programs, flexible budgeting, and brain trusts. Technology opens the world through random meet-ups, large-scale events, videoconferencing, messaging apps, and collaborative technology platforms. Pick any tool and experiment with it. And if it doesn't catch on immediately, remember the flywheel metaphor: keep trying. With gentle but relentless pressure, you'll gain momentum and establish a culture of asking, giving, and receiving across boundaries.

REFLECTIONS AND ACTIONS

1. How easy or hard is it for you or members of your organization to ask across internal boundaries or external boundaries? Why?

2. To what extent are organizational silos a problem in your organization?

3. Where is the low-hanging fruit—places where bridging silos would yield big benefits?

4. Which organizational practice would be best suited to capitalize on the opportunity you identified in #3? (You might consider using more than one tool.)

5. Which technology would help to ask across boundaries?

6. Run the experiment! Don't quit, keep trying, and persist to get the flywheel turning.

CHAPTER 7

RECOGNITION AND REWARDS

When I was a greenhorn assistant professor, focused on publishing research, I occasionally ran into statistics problems that I didn't know how to solve, or an odd statistical procedure that I was unfamiliar with. I knew some things about statistics, but I wasn't exactly a world-class statistician. At one point, I got so stuck that I decided to find an expert on the faculty and asked him for help. He answered my question, but only after rolling his eyes and commenting, "I thought *everyone* learned that in graduate school. I guess you didn't." I got the solution I needed, but I felt so deflated by his comment that I couldn't work on the project for days after.

The next time I needed help on a problem, I turned to him again, figuring that he must have simply been having a bad day on that previous occasion. This time, when I asked him my question, he sighed and said, "*Everyone* knows that that's in the *bible* of statistics." Then he pulled a fat tome off his shelves and tossed it to me. As before, I got my answer, and my ego got a bruising in the process.

Twice burned, thrice shy. I found another expert to ask for help.

His reaction couldn't have been more different. "Now, *that's* an interesting question!" he said. He then explained why it was interesting and worked with me to find the solution. This time, I left with the help I needed *and* the motivation to do something with it. I returned a few more times, and each time the experience was positive, and reinforced our collegial rapport. Eventually, we collaborated on a research project and coauthored a publication in a top academic journal.

In our society, the act of giving help is almost always recognized and rewarded, whether in the form of gratitude, elevated status, or some quid pro quo. But what about *asking* for help? Some might argue that simply getting the help we ask for is its own reward. But as my story shows, not all help is equal. The *how*—how our request is received, how we are treated, and how the help is granted— determines whether we get discouraged, or encouraged to make asking a personal practice.

That's why recognizing, appreciating, and rewarding those who ask is as critical as doing the same for those who answer. In this chapter, I describe some practices, both formal and informal, that reinforce the giving-receiving cycle. I show how teams and companies can benefit from rewarding both giving *and* taking, and how these practices can support and strengthen the tools you've learned about in the previous chapters.

THE POWER OF RECOGNITION AT WORK

Think of a time when you were recognized for a great accomplishment. It might have been a boss, coach, teacher, or parent who praised you. Take a moment, close your eyes, and relive the experience.

How do you feel?

I'm sure the memory brings back good feelings, because recognition is a fundamental human need. Recognition tells us that we are valued, that we belong, that we are included, accepted, and appreciated. We are motivated by recognition and demotivated by the lack of it. And studies show that recognition produces countless benefits in the workplace.[1] Those who feel recognized are more engaged, more productive, and more satisfied at work; they exert more effort; they are more trusting and more excited about the prospects of change; and they are less likely to quit, in part because they are more likely to believe that their leaders want to build a positive and humane workplace in which employee well-being is paramount.[2] Receiving praise even elevates dopamine levels in the brain, which produces positive emotions.

Sadly, over 20 percent of full-time employees in the United States report that they *never* receive recognition for their contributions at work, according to a survey by the Globoforce Workplace Research Institute.[3] An additional 30 percent say they have not been recognized in the past six months or more. That means that a large number of employers forgo the many benefits of creating a culture where employees feel appreciated for what they do.

"When people don't get enough recognition, they ask

themselves, 'What am I doing this for? Nobody cares,'"
says David Grazian, the former vice president and director
of corporate taxation at Granite Construction, Inc., a $3
billion civil construction company headquartered in California that *Forbes* rates as one of the 100 Most Trustwor-
thy Companies in America.[4] "People want recognition; they
want to be noticed and appreciated," David says.[5]

People can be recognized for so many things: for using
their strengths and skills effectively, for their achievements and accomplishments, and for their contributions
to the organization's objectives, mission, and vision.[6] In
this chapter, however, I focus specifically on recognition
that motivates asking for and giving help. And while most
practices you'll read about in this chapter are originally
designed to appreciate *giving,* not *asking,* they can all be
adapted to recognize those who ask for what they need as
well. Often, all it takes is a shift of perspective.

THANKS FOR ASKING!

Every day we are surrounded by opportunities to appreciate people when they give help *and* when they ask for it.
The best kind of recognition is that which is frequent, and
repeated—which is why informal, everyday recognition is
so effective. "Formal praise exercises only work so long—
they have a short shelf life," David Grazian notes. "In my
opinion, appreciation and interest have to be exhibited on
a regular basis in normal interactions. People need a day-
to-day feeling of being appreciated and recognized for what
they do."

Yet to be effective, that recognition must be authentic.

"Authentic recognition causes people to be appreciated, to feel whole, to feel that they contribute," says Kevin Ames, director of O.C. Tanner Institute, a global recognition and engagement firm, and coauthor of *Appreciate: Celebrating People, Inspiring Greatness*.[7] We have sensitive antennae for inauthenticity. Recognition programs and practices fall flat if they aren't used to give authentic recognition.

Candice Billups is a custodian who has worked at the University of Michigan hospitals for over thirty years. Her job in the cancer center is to strip and wax floors; clean restrooms; restock toilet paper, tissues, and paper towels; and clean up chemo spills or after a patient throws up or becomes incontinent. If you ask Candice, she'll tell you that her job is public relations. She talks with the patients, tells jokes and makes them laugh, acts as a confidante, and comforts them. "I love my patients," says Candice. "I love them all. When I go home, I feel very fulfilled."[8] Top leaders at the hospital have authentically recognized Candice; for example, they sent a detailed memo about her to all hospital personnel, praising her superlative dedication and service.

Many companies use some combination of formal and informal recognition, plus a system of compensation, perks, or other material rewards, to motivate people to do the right thing. Psychologists of motivation used to worry that providing extrinsic motivators like recognition and rewards undermines, or "crowds out," intrinsic motivators, like the personal satisfaction we draw from our work. Well, that certainly isn't the case for Candice, and in fact a giant meta-analysis of forty years of scientific studies on this topic concludes that intrinsic motivation remains a medium-to-strong predictor of performance even in the presence of monetary rewards.[9] Intrinsic and extrinsic motivators coexist in every work situation, and to create an authentic culture of contribution, the best approach is to find a workable balance between them.

You can add recognition routines to any team tool (see Chapter 5), or to any organizational practice or technology that asks across boundaries (see Chapter 6). Words of recognition could be a shout-out to the entire team ("Thanks, everyone, for the requests you made today!") or delivered one-to-one ("I appreciate the ask you made today. That's an important issue and we'll all learn from you."). The preflight phase of a new team is an opportunity to establish recognition—for both asking and giving—as the norm. ("We know that asking for help is just as critical to our success as giving help. Let's be sure to appreciate those who ask for help *and* those who provide it.") And the post-flight phase is an opportunity to look back and ask, "Did we recognize and appreciate those who asked for help as well as gave it? What did we do well, and what can we do better next time?"

WHAT'S THE BEST WAY TO RECOGNIZE PEOPLE?

Deborah was one of the best administrative assistants I've ever had. When I talked with her, she gave me her undivided attention. When I requested she do something, she was 100 percent reliable. I never had to worry that something wouldn't get done on time or would fall through the cracks. Often, she would even anticipate a need and respond to it before I asked. She was this way with everyone, and we wanted to recognize her for it. We got a bouquet of flowers and a gift card, planning to present them publicly in front of the entire office staff. When she caught wind of our plans, she was so mortified, she almost fled the building. That's when we realized our mistake: she was a quiet, shy, introverted person who generally hated being the center of attention. It made perfect sense that public recognition would feel like punishment rather than a reward. Fortunately, we figured this out in time, presenting the flowers and gift card to her in a small, quiet, informal gathering at her desk.

"What's the best way to recognize people?" is a trick question. There isn't one best way. The ways in which people like (and dislike) to be recognized are many and varied. It's important to look at each person as an individual and take his or her personality into account. Would this person want a big public display of appreciation, or would they prefer it expressed verbally one-on-one? Would they be more comfortable with a written note, phone call, Post-it, email, or text, or would a certificate of appreciation, an appreciative note in a newsletter, or an announcement in a meeting or at an event make their day? For recognition to be meaningful, the content should also be personalized to the recipient.[10] "I've continued to learn that praise means more when it's specific," says Ari Weinzweig, co-founder and CEO of Zingerman's Community of Businesses.[11] "While general thanks and kudos never hurt," he says, "it's more helpful to be clear about what is it that we really value, so that others know what they can do more of down the road to be even more effective in their work." Personalized recognition shows that you are paying attention to what people value and find meaningful.

My literary agent Jim Levine, who you read about in

Chapter 5, told me how recognizing people for asking created a breakthrough for his agency. Despite the agency's written guidelines that explicitly encourage asking, a developmental review with Cristela, the assistant to the business manager, revealed that she had not been asking for the help she needed. When Jim and his partners asked if perhaps they hadn't made it clear that they want everyone in the office to speak up when they need something, she said, "Yes, you've been clear. But as you know, I'm very shy."

Jim always makes the extra effort to recognize people's contribution one-on-one and in bi-weekly staff meetings. But suddenly he realized that he hadn't been recognizing people for "asking," because he assumed it was so baked into the agency culture. At the next staff meeting, he made it a point to give people shout-outs by name for asking questions.

As you can imagine, it was gratifying when shortly thereafter Cristela came to him and the other partners asking them for a "larger role" in the agency's work. Victoria, a senior agent, suggested letting Cristela cut her teeth on some editorial work, like reviewing manuscripts. Cristela's reviews turned out to be fabulous: greatly appreciated by Victoria and Jim, as well as by their client-authors, and they are continuing to expand her role in the editorial review process.

The lesson? Even if you think you are cultivating a culture that fosters asking, you may need to take extra steps to reach specific individuals and extra steps to make sure that regular communications reinforce the encouragement of and recognition for asking.

A shout-out at the end of a stand-up, huddle, cross-collaboration workshop, or a large-scale event is a simple way to informally recognize the requesting that took place. And it's even easier to recognize or praise requests made in random meet-ups, messaging apps, or collaborative technology platforms. For example, when I receive a request from a student via email, I usually start my return message with "Thanks for asking!" In Givitas, I've seen "Thanks for posting!" as the first line in many responses to people's requests. And recognition can of course be given in person, as it was for me in the case of the second statistics expert who told me *"That's* an interesting question!" Such informal recognitions remind everyone that not only is it okay to ask for help, but that asking is actually encouraged.

Another practice is "Pennies in Your Pocket," developed by professional coach Marian J. Their.[12] As Dani Fankhauser, director of content marking at Reflektive, described the exercise in a blog post for Give and Take, Inc., in the morning simply put ten pennies in your right pocket.[13] During the day, look for people to appreciate. For each expression of appreciation, transfer one penny to your left pocket. The goal is to have all the pennies in your left pocket by the time you leave for the evening. Practices like Pennies in Your Pocket elevate your awareness and attention; they alert you to the daily opportunities that surround you to recognize people who ask for and give help.

GRATITUDE WALLS

The Center for Positive Organizations (CPO) uses the tool Sugar Cubes to recognize both giving and receiving. "Sugar Cubes" refers to a set of colorful envelopes strung on a clothesline in the hallway; each member of the CPO community has an envelope. Students, staff, faculty, and even visitors use the envelopes to share notes of gratitude and congratulations and, in some cases, offers of help.

Every Friday during the school year, a group of fifty university students gather with staff and scholars at a CPO workshop. Each meeting begins with participants going around the room and sharing something good that happened that week. During one workshop, a student named Dan (not his real name) cited "making it through the week."[14] Then he went on to describe a week of non-stop disappointments—bad recruiting news, difficult team dynamics, and conflict with his longtime partner. Betsy Erwin, senior associate director and education lead, heard this as a plea for help. "In my former life," Betsy told me, "I worked in MBA career services. So, I thought I could be helpful to Dan." Betsy put a note in his Sugar Cubes envelope letting him know that she appreciated him sharing details of his bad week and that she was available to chat if he wanted her advice. Though Dan had been initially a little reluctant to ask for and accept help with his woes, Betsy's note thanking him for sharing gave him the encouragement he needed. "A week later, and a few times after that," Betsy said, "we met for coffee and career counseling."

Sugar Cubes is a tool that Chris White, CPO managing director, learned when he participated as a student in AIE-SEC, a global platform dedicated to developing youth leaders. Originally used to express sweet sentiments (hence the name), Sugar Cubes is one example of what is called generally a "gratitude wall." The gratitude wall is a common recognition practice that can take various forms. At

Hopelab, the social innovation lab I told you about in Chapter 6, blank "thank you" cards are displayed on a wall; any staffer who wishes to express gratitude takes a card, writes a note, and either delivers it to the person or sticks it back on the wall. Research shows that expressing gratitude has positive short-term and long-term effects on those who give and those who receive gratitude, and that gratitude fuels the cycle of giving and receiving.[15] You can use a gratitude wall to appreciate those who help *and* those who ask for help.

FORMAL RECOGNITION PROGRAMS

The sky's the limit—literally—when it comes to creative ways to recognize people. Soon after my former PhD student Kathryn Dekas began working at Google, her team manager expressed his appreciation for the team's hard work by treating them to an afternoon of indoor skydiving: a rather ingenious activity that lets people experience the rush of skydiving by leaping into a vertical wind tunnel and "flying" on a column of air. Kathryn is now head of Google's People Innovation Lab (known as PiLab), and her skydiving experience is just one example of the many ways Google recognizes its employees.

Beyond the wacky excursions (and the parties, spa or resort visits, and so on), Google also has a host of formal recognition programs and tools typically used to recognize giving, but that can just as easily be used to recognize asking.[16] gThanks ("gee-thanks"), which makes it easy for employees to send one another thank-you notes, is one of them. "You just enter someone's name, hit 'kudos' and then type up a note," explains Laszlo Bock, former senior vice president of people at Google.[17] The recipient's manager is automatically notified, and the kudos are made public, so anyone in the company can see them. Bock has even been known to post hard copies of kudos given to members of his team on the "Wall of Happy" in his office, just for good measure.[18] The peer bonus option in gThanks encourages Googlers to recognize their peers who went above and beyond the call of duty. The recipient gets a standard cash award of $175. The recipient's manager is notified, but prior management approval isn't necessary to grant a peer bonus. Managers also award spot bonuses to employees who have made a big impact on the business. The bigger the impact, the bigger the bonus, says Mary Beth Heine, a Google compensation specialist.[19]

Practices like these aren't unique to Google. In fact, more than 80 percent of U.S. organizations have employee recognition programs, and they come in many colors and flavors.[20] Consider, for example, the High-5 program developed by Algentis, an HR outsourcing firm in the San Francisco Bay area that is now part of HUB International. This program allowed any employee to give any other employee a High-5—a $25 Amazon gift card—for "going above and beyond to help them out," says Alexis Haselberger, whom you met in Chapter 5. A High-5 didn't need management approval, and each person could award up to two High-5s per month. "High-5s really increased the collaboration between teams," says Alexis, "and made visible people who were really helping out their coworkers." It's easy to see how awarding High-5s to those who *ask* for help would have a positive impact on collaboration and teamwork as well.

A tech start-up in Boston has a formal values nominations program that recognizes team members who help their teammates. Every Friday, everyone gets an email request for nominations. Anyone can nominate anyone, and the CEO includes all the nominations in a Sunday email message to the company. Nominations are also added to a "values" channel in Slack. Research shows that recognition programs tied to a company's core values are more effective than recognition programs that are not.[21] So, why not make asking a core value and recognize those who do it?

The formal recognition tools I've mentioned so far are homegrown, but there also exist plenty of ready-made recognition platforms. For example, O.C. Tanner provides a suite of recognition and reward tools, with more than thirteen million users worldwide. Reward Gateway, Halo Recognition, Bonusly, and other third-party platforms have features and functions to provide peer bonuses, kudos, celebrations, and more. Cook Inlet Region, Inc. (CIRI) in Anchorage, Alaska, uses KudosNow, a peer-to-peer social recognition platform similar in concept to Google's gThanks. "We try to find ways to recognize someone who lives our values," explains Molly Webb, a senior manager for human resources at the company.[22] Each month, the Rewards and Recognition Committee comes up with a different challenge—like "honor and respect," for example. Perhaps CIRI will one day create a monthly challenge centered around asking!

GTB, a global media firm, uses the platform You EarnedIt! (YEI) for its peer bonus system. With offices and field locations around the globe, they find that this tool makes it easy for anyone to recognize someone anywhere. Kiran Chaudhri Lenz, director, business operations program management, says, "YEI is very equitable, very visible."[23] Recognition translates into points that a recipient can redeem for gift certificates, charitable donations, or company swag. Some employees, says Kiran, even use their points to buy more points to recognize others. Like all the tools I've described, YEI can be used to recognize both asking and giving help. Doing so doesn't mean reprogramming the system; YEI points could simply be awarded for good questions and requests.

THE MOUNTAIN MAN AND THE WAGON TRAIN

Ravi couldn't help but feel a twinge of jealousy as he bid his colleague "bon voyage." The next day, she was embarking on an all-expense paid trip to Hawaii; she had recently topped the sales leaderboard and won the trip as a perk.[24] But Ravi knew that a significant portion of her spectacular sales numbers came from the lucrative lead he had shared with her. The company encouraged salespeople to exchange leads and help each other, but it hadn't come up with a way for them to share the rewards.

Ravi's story is an example of a common problem known as "the folly of rewarding A, while hoping for B."[25] His company claimed to want to encourage cooperation among its salespeople, but by rewarding individual performance, it was in fact creating competition. Unfortunately, this problem is not rare. My colleague John Tropman, a compensation specialist, calls it the mountain man and the wagon train.[26] The mountain man or woman is a rugged individualist who lives or dies on their own. The wagon train is a caravan of settlers who band together, increasing the odds of survival by cooperating with one another. Many compensation systems, John explains, reward the mountain man or woman, when in reality effective teams and companies operate as wagon trains.

Fortunately, it is possible to keep this folly in check by implementing systems that authentically reward the behaviors you hope for.

Agile Performance Management

When Deloitte—the world's largest professional services firm—ditched its traditional performance management system, it also tossed its annual rituals of beginning-of-year goal-setting and end-of-year reviews.[27] Other companies are doing the same.[28] The traditional approach to performance management—one more focused on accountability for past results than on performance improvement in the future—was inconsistent, time-consuming, and out of step with the need for speed and agility. By the end of the year, looking back on goals set at the beginning was "like looking at an old photo album," says Erica Bank, performance leader at Deloitte.[29] You recognize the picture, but it's out-of-date. So, Deloitte set about replacing the old system with one that would reflect the actual pace and rhythm of work.

Deloitte's work is project-based, so at the end of each project, the project manager or leader records a quick "performance snapshot" for each team member. This snapshot consists of four survey questions and comments.[30] These capture the value of the person's work, and how the person works to obtain results; they also identify people who are ready for promotion, or who are at risk for low performance and would benefit from corrective action.

Typically, a person has seven to twelve performance snapshots a year, says Erica. The highest so far is forty-two. For work that is not project-based, performance snapshots are taken four times a year. The results of each individual snapshot are not shared with the person; but at least once or as many as four times a year, the person will see a scatter-plot that shows where the person is relative to many other people. This becomes the basis of conversations with the leader about what the person is doing right and where he or she needs to improve or change behavior. For example, the person might be coached to ask for help more often, rather than going it alone.

Check-ins are another new feature of the system. Every week or two, a professional is expected to ask their leader for a short conversation about current and near-term work; the leader never initiates. The check-in "normalizes asking," says Erica. It's an "organizational blessing that it's okay to ask for attention, or feedback, or help." For example, a professional might reach out to their manager to request a check-in by saying, "I have a big client meeting coming up, and I need help."

By the end of the year, compensation decisions are made with performance data that were captured in real time throughout the year. These data include the performance snapshots, metrics such as utilization or sales made, and other activities that the professional might have done on behalf of the firm, such as leading a seminar or teaching a class. The result, says Erica, is a much more nuanced conversation about ongoing performance and compensation that factors in collaboration and teamwork, as well as quantitative results.

"Zero Dark Thirty"—and Other Mini-Games for Shared Rewards and Profit

"We need more customer complaints!" exclaimed Ron Maurer, chief administrative officer of Zingerman's Community of Businesses (ZCoB). Ron heads Zingerman's Service Network (ZSN), which is responsible for providing shared services—human resources, technology, marketing, finance, accounting, web, and more—to all ZCoB businesses. These businesses are ZSN's customers and getting more complaints from them was the objective of a ZSN mini-game. A mini-game is a fun, small-scale, short-term exercise designed to incentivize people to fix a problem or capitalize on an opportunity. The purpose of ZSN's mini-game wasn't to generate complaints by making more mistakes, of course, but rather to learn what ZSN was or wasn't doing that *caused* complaints, and then fix it.

The typical practice in a business is to wait for compliments and ignore complaints. But ZSN decided to use the mini-game—which they named "Get Merry with Green & Red" because it was played for ten weeks over the holidays—to be proactive. ZSN "players" were sent to visit the weekly huddles held in all ZCoB businesses, with the assignment to ask for and document both compliments (code greens) and complaints (code reds)—and then take action to address them. The mini-game design specified three levels of performance based on the number of greens and reds submitted and the number of process improvements instituted; rewards were attached to each (see game details in the appendix). Reaching level 3 in ten weeks, for example, earned each person $150. What is significant about this game isn't the rewards themselves, it's how they are awarded: not based on individual performance, but rather on outcomes achieved by the team. Winnings were shared, so that everyone earned the cash bonus, or no one did. In other words, the mini-game was designed to incentivize players to cooperate, and disincentivize them to compete.

John Kohl, CEO of Atlas Wholesale Food Company, employed a similar strategy at his three-generation family business. He'll be the first to tell you that the first mini-game, which he designed, was a flop. It should have worked, but his employees just didn't get behind it. John soon understood the issue: people support what they create. So, from then on, he asked his employees to design their own mini-games, subject to his sign-off.

The opportunity sparked an explosion of imagination and creativity. For example, employees designed "Zero Dark Thirty: The Quest to Assassinate Errors" to reduce the number of picking errors during the night shift (which result in incorrect orders being shipped). As with "Get Merry," winnings were "all for one and one for all"—either all players would win the prize (their choice of a set of power tools or a deluxe toolbox), or no one would. This mini-game reduced picking errors by 37 percent in just four weeks. And the improvement persisted well after the four weeks were over.

The great thing about mini-games is that they can be used to incentivize just about anything.[31] ShopBot Tools, Inc., makers of CNC (computer numerically controlled) cutting tools, devised a mini-game to get more social media attention. Named "#Hippies," players earned three "brownies" for posting original content and one for reposting content. The team could win an actual brownie party for earning a hundred "brownies" in thirty days, tie-dye T-shirts for three hundred in sixty days, and a skating party for six hundred in ninety days. Most of the employees are hourly workers and didn't have social media accounts or know how to use them, so a lot of people asked things like "'How do I set up my account? How do I use it? How do I post or repost?' And so on," recalls Anne-Claire Broughton, who advises ShopBot. A lot of help was asked for and given to win the game—and win they did, earning all three prizes.

Asking for help wasn't the main purpose of the ShopBot mini-game, but without asking, it was almost impossible to win. The same is true for every mini-game. Mini-games are a means by which a team seeks and discovers the root causes of a problem or the best way to take advantage of an opportunity. Along the way, mini-game players have to ask for a lot of help, from team members as well as across boundaries, because the information, resources, or expertise you need often are outside the team. Team members ask questions, make requests, and work together to conceptualize, design, play, and win a mini-game.[32]

How might a mini-game look if it were designed *explicitly* to increase asking? We know it would follow the same design guidelines that every mini-game uses: know and teach the rules, keep score, and share the success. (See the appendix for detailed mini-game design guidelines.) Let's say, for example, that the goal was to incentivize fundraising for a good cause—something that by definition requires a lot of asks. The team could be challenged to raise a specified amount of money by a specified deadline, and if the team meets or exceeds its goal, the reward could be a celebration, a party, and so on.

Another approach would be to use one of the collaborative technology platforms (see Chapter 6) as the vehicle for playing a mini-game. The built-in metrics in these platforms make it easy to keep score. Givitas, for example, provides individual and group metrics, such as how many requests and how many offers each person makes, and group totals. Suppose, for example, that the team is working on a complex project that requires members to collaborate with one another, providing opportunities to ask for advice, ideas, support, information, or other resources to accomplish it. The mini-game could make the total number of requests—such as "Does anyone know someone who has information on X?" "I need a quick review of a memo, could anyone help?" "I need to brainstorm about an issue—who can huddle up with me in fifteen minutes?"—a group metric and the rewards could be a team celebration or a set dollar amount. As with any mini-game, the people who will play should be the ones to design it, subject to the leader's sign-off. People support what they create, and if you give them the opportunity, they will come up with something truly creative.

The Great Game of Business

In the early 1980s, Springfield Remanufacturing Corporation (SRC) teetered on the edge of bankruptcy. Remanufacturing is a complex and collaborative process that involves rebuilding a product—in this case, parts and equipment for agricultural, industrial, construction, and transportation markets—using a combination of reused, repaired, and new parts. CEO Jack Stack saw that profitability was lagging to the point that bankruptcy was right around the corner, but he couldn't seem to figure out how to turn things around. That is, until he conceived of the idea of business as a game—albeit a serious one—with rules, scores, and shared outcomes. To win, everyone would have to think and act like owners, understanding how operations impact the financials and generate profit, tracking performance, and helping one another to maximize financial gains that would be shared among all team members. This approach rescued the company, and Jack and SRC built the idea out into a system of innovative practices now known as the Great Game of Business.[33] Today, the company is SRC Holdings, one of *Forbes'* Top 25 Best Small Companies in America, with multiple businesses and annual revenues of $600 million. Over 10,000 companies have adopted SRC's methodology in one form or another.

I visited SRC in Springfield, Missouri, to see firsthand how the system works. At SRC Electrical (SRCE), I observed more than one hundred workers assembled for their weekly huddle; each worker seated at the table had a binder of financial and operational documents and a calculator. The room's walls were covered with large whiteboards displaying SRCE's balance sheet, income statement, gainsharing, and more. All numbers were current, updated from the week before. Workers knew exactly where the business was financially and operationally—and, perhaps most important, they could track their progress toward reaching their shared goals. SRCE's managers and workers led the meeting; while reviewing the numbers, if there were variances from expectations, they didn't point fingers but instead discussed the story behind the shortfall to figure out what happened and how to fix it. Armed with this information, they could make weekly corrections in their work. And with their goals and personal outcomes aligned, they were highly incentivized to ask for and offer help.

SRC keeps regular wages and salaries at levels that ensure job security if people do good work.[34] "But if people do a better than decent job," Jack says, "if they can figure out ways to improve, the company shares with them whatever additional money they generate by paying them bonuses. The more they generate, the bigger the bonuses."[35] (See the appendix for more information on how gainsharing calculations work.)

The gainsharing program makes business a team sport, encouraging cooperation over competition, and making asking for and giving help critical to winning. "It ensures that everyone has the same priorities and that we all stay focused on the same goals," says Jack.[36] "When one department is having trouble, another department will send in reinforcements, and everybody understands why. Often people don't even have to be asked. They will help each other out spontaneously, sometimes at great inconvenience. That's because the program makes everyone aware of how much we depend on one another to hit our targets. We win together or we don't win at all."

SUMMARY

Recognition and rewards are powerful motivators in the workplace. When used properly, they strengthen the effectiveness of the tools and practices I described in the preceding chapters. Appreciating those who ask for what they need—through authentic, personalized praise and recognition—is an essential ingredient of the asking-giving-receiving cycle. A host of informal practices and formal recognition programs are available and can be tailored to specific needs. Compensation systems and mini-games can also be used to encourage asking and helping behavior, if designed in such a way that everyone shares in the rewards.

REFLECTIONS & ACTIONS

1. How do you like to be recognized? How do others around you like to be recognized?
2. In your workplace, are people who ask for help recognized and rewarded—or criticized and punished?
3. Look for opportunities to thank people for asking— one-to-one, in teams or groups, or after using the tools and practices in the preceding chapters.
4. Make it a habit to record the details of someone you observed making an effective request or a generous offer of help. Then refer to these notes when you want to recognize someone for asking or giving.
5. If you have formal recognition programs at work, use them to appreciate those who ask and what they ask for.

6. Propose and work with others to design a mini-game to incentivize cooperation, asking for, and giving help in your team or within your organization.

7. As a manager or leader, make asking for help a performance competency, and reward those who ask.

8. Use gainsharing programs to share the rewards of asking for, giving, and receiving help.

APPENDIX

MINI-GAME DESIGN FOR "GET MERRY WITH GREEN & RED" AT ZINGERMAN'S SERVICE NETWORK

Game Name: "Get Merry with Green & Red"

Game Description:

The holidays are all about green and red colors. So, why not focus on our Zplan goals of increasing our Code Reds and Code Greens to help improve our business. And let's take it up a notch from there by taking solid and forward-thinking actions on them. This effort is meant to help us get better at getting involved in this process, as well as taking action on issues that are raised so that we can do a better job for ourselves, our departments, the entire ZNET, and all of ZCoB.

Level 1—A combined total of Code Greens and Code Reds submitted within ZSN will be double the year plan of twelve. Each person is responsible for submitting *at least* one Code Green and one Code Red so that we result in at least twenty-four for our year actual.

Level 2—Implement five systemic process improvements based on submitted Code Greens or Code Reds from Level 1. The process improvement must be Workin' worthy, as an article announcing our results will be posted in the February edition of Workin'.

Level 3—Implement fifteen systemic process improvements (ten in addition to the five in Level 2) based on submitted Code Greens or Code Reds from Level 1. The process improvement must be Workin' worthy, as in Level 2.

The Game has the following rules:

- The game runs from November 20–January 31 (10 weeks).
- Only Code Greens & Code Reds related specifically to ZSN qualify.
- Each person is responsible for documenting, communicating, and implementing.

Keeping Score:

We will review progress on this game by monitoring the Code Reds/Greens submitted and reviewing actions being taken.

Sharing the winnings:

It's all for one and one for all, we either make it or we don't!

Rewards:

Level 1–$20 Zingerman's gift card

Level 2–$75—each person can choose either a Zingerman's gift card, ZBucks, or paycheck earnings.

Level 3–$150—each person can choose either a Zinger-man's gift card, ZBucks, or paycheck earnings.

The max reward is $150 total.

If we reach Level 2, we bypass the $20 and get $75.

If we reach Level 3, we bypass the $20 and $75 and get $150.

MINI-GAME DESIGN FOR "ZERO DARK THIRTY" AT ATLAS WHOLESALE FOOD COMPANY

Game Name: Zero Dark Thirty: The Quest to Assassinate Errors

Goal: Less than thirty picking errors over the course of ninety days, or three five-day streaks with *no* errors.

Business Goal: To increase our overall level of customer satisfaction by picking perfect orders for our drivers to deliver.

Time Frame: Ninety days

Rules: Every order is picked and stickered with 100 percent accuracy. Every day with *no* products stickered with the incorrect label or a product short on a driver's truck will count as "error free." All errors are subject to management judgment. Every picking error will reduce the chart by one error. There must be at least one error left on the chart by June 28, or three streaks of five no-error days will also qualify.

Players: All Pickers and warehouse staff who put inventory away.

Scoreboard: Every consecutive day with no picking/warehouse errors will be kept track of on a whiteboard in the front office. There will also be a board with thirty errors on it. We will tear down one sheet for every error.

Meetings: Results, process improvements, and ideas will be shared daily. Any errors will be posted in the front office to review.

Reward: Choice of a totally awesome set of power tools or a deluxe toolbox with fasteners.

MINI-GAME DESIGN GUIDELINES

Definition

A mini-game is a small-scale incentive plan designed to fix a problem or capitalize on an opportunity. It is a short, motivating, and fun way to make improvements.

Three Rules of Designing a Mini-Game

1. Know and teach the rules
2. Keep score on a fun scoreboard
3. Share the success

Step 1. What are the key issues you want to address in your organization?

- Choose your focus
- What bottom-line results are at issue?
- What key number are you targeting?
- Think narrow, not broad
- Choose metrics with only a few drivers

- Who is playing the game?
- How long will the game be played?
- How will you check the viability of the game?
- Math checks and sign-offs
- Any de-motivators?
- Any unintended consequences?

Step 2. How will we keep score?

- What is scored?
- Who will keep score?
- What's a fun scoreboard?

Step 3. How do we measure success?

- What is the benefit to the organization?
- How will you calculate who gets what?
- Cash rewards?
- Symbolic rewards, celebrations?
- Prizes? (should be motivating and memorable)

Sources: Greatgame.com & ZingTrain.com

GAINSHARING CALCULATIONS AT ATLAS WHOLESALE FOOD COMPANY

CEO John Kohl implemented the gainsharing model developed by the Great Game of Business. Instead of an annual bonus, bonuses are calculated each quarter and paid if they are earned. This gives employees the opportunity to win early and to keep winning. And it ties what they do more closely to what they earn.

If employees don't earn the bonus in one quarter, any unearned bonus rolls over to the next quarter, so they still have the opportunity to earn the entire bonus. Even if they missed the first three bonus targets, they could still make it all up by the end of the year. This arrangement keeps people motivated and engaged throughout the year. For more details, see *The Great Game of Business* by Jack Stack with Bo Burlingham.

Payout Level

| Annual Employee Salary | X | Critical Number | | X | Quarterly Payouts | | = | Quarterly Bonus $$$$ |

Payout Level

Critical Number	
Net Profit	% of Salary
1.50%	1.0%
1.75%	2.5%
2.00%	4.0%
2.25%	5.5%
3.0%	7.0%

Quarterly Payouts

Quarter	% of Bonus
Q1	10%
Q2	20%
Q3	30%
Q4	40%

Annual Employee Salary X [Payout Level] X [Quarterly Payouts] = Quarterly Bonus $$$$

ACKNOWLEDGMENTS

I asked a lot of people for help with this book.

The project began with a short manuscript of preliminary ideas and examples, and I asked Michael Arena, Cheryl Baker, Larry Freed, Kurt Riegger, and Chris White to look it over. I am grateful to them for helpful comments and suggestions on this early version, all of which encouraged me to embark on writing this book.

When it came time to find a literary agent, I asked my colleague and business partner Adam Grant for recommendations. He put me in touch with Jim Levine of Levine Greenberg Rostan Literary Agency. It was a perfect match, and I am grateful to Adam for making it happen. Jim and I hit it off immediately. Jim's leadership philosophy resonates with the message of this book (you'll see some of his wisdom in it). I thank Jim for his faithful support of this book and sage guidance throughout the publishing process and beyond.

The ideal agent leads to the ideal publisher and that was the case for me when Jim connected me with Currency/Penguin Random House. I am grateful for the depth of support that Currency has afforded me and this book. I especially acknowledge Talia Krohn, editor extraordinaire, who worked with me from start to finish, bringing the book up to a level I could not have achieved alone. I appreciate Pam Feinstein for deft copyediting. I thank the entire team at Currency for their expertise and dedication, including Tina Constable, Campbell Wharton, Andrea DeWerd, Steven Boriack, Nicole McArdle, Nick Stewart, and Erin Little.

This may seem odd, but I am also grateful for the Givitas collaborative technology platform we created at our company, Give and Take, Inc. I made many requests to various Givitas communities, asking for examples and best practices to illustrate the theme of this book. Many you'll read about came from people I didn't know before, yet who generously responded to my requests. For developing Givitas and building the business, I thank the entire team at Give and Take, Inc.: Sarah Allen-Short, Cheryl Baker, Katie Bennett, Larry Freed, Dave Jansen, Gal Katz, Krystie Lee, Nikki Marton, Amber Varacalli, and Matt Wenner.

I gratefully acknowledge the staff, students, and faculty at our Center for Positive Organizations (CPO). Our staff lives on a daily basis the principles we teach: Angie Ceely, Betsy Erwin, Jacob Feinberg, Esther Kyte, Emily Penix, Stacey Scimeca, and Katie Trevathan. I am grateful for continuously learning from my CPO core faculty colleagues over so many years: Kim Cameron, Jane Dutton, Mari

Kira, Shirli Kopelman, Julia Lee, Dave Mayer, Bob Quinn, Gretchen Spreitzer, and Amy Young. Our students are too many to mention by name, but I acknowledge them all for their journeys as positive leaders.

I benefited from expert research assistance and library support. I thank Sarah Gordon, doctoral candidate in our program, for combing the web and her networks to find new examples and cases for me; doctoral candidate Hilary Hendricks for helping me to develop the Asking-Giving assessment you'll find in Chapter 3; Lillian Chen, senior research consultant and research manager at the Ross School, for providing technical expertise; and Corey Seeman, director, Kresge library services, for helping me secure permissions to reproduce material. To this note of thanks, I add faculty coordinators Karen Phelps and Janine Amadi, and information associate Shovonne Pearson, for responding quickly and cheerfully to what must seem like an endless supply of urgent requests from me.

As always, I am thankful for the institutional and financial support of the Ross School of Business and the University of Michigan.

One of the delights of writing this book is that it gave me so many opportunities to connect with and learn from former and current students and colleagues, and to meet many new people in the process of researching and writing. For contributing their ideas, insights, examples, and other materials, I thank: Lauren Acquista, Ach Adhvaryu, Cheri Alexander, Sarah Allen-Short, Janine Amadi, Randy Alpert, Kevin Ames, Laav Anandan, Susan Ashford, Harrison Baker, Erica Bank, Lynn Bartlett, Maggie Bayless, Jim Best, Kevin Blue, Anne-Claire Broughton, Lindsay Cameron, Tom Caprel, Paula Caproni, Dan Cawley, Rob

Cross, Jerry Davis, Kathryn Dekas, Jeff DeGraff, Jane Dutton, Amy Edmondson, Daniel Eisenberg, Betsy Erwin, Joe Ferstle, Megan Finley, Dani Fankhauser, Dave Grazian, Leslie Gray, Fernanda Gregorio, Ted Hall, Scott Hanton, Alexis Haselberger, Mary Beth Heine, Wally Hopp, Heather Currier Hunt, Christina Keller, Fred Keller, Meghan Kiesel, Ji Hye Kim, John Kohl, Shirli Kopelman, Mijeong Kwon, Julia Lee, Sheen Levine, Kiran Chaudhri Lenz, Jim Mallozzi, Ron May, Dave Mayer, Ron Maurer, Kusuma Mopury, Abby Murray, Mawa Mustafa, Prabjot Nanua, Tom Paider, Alyssa Patzius, Dan Ranta, Andrew Radvansky, Brian Rodriquez, Dave Scholten, Don Sexton, Rich Sheridan, David Sherman, Rich Smalling, Salvador Salort-Pons, Felicia Solomon, Gretchen Spreitzer, Laura Sonday, Andrew Stocking, Noel Tichy, John Tropman, Ryan Quinn, Shawn Quinn, Jose Uribe, Matt Van Nortwick, Molly Webb, Ari Weinzwieg, Chad Weldy, Chris White, and Tony Wydra.

I always save the most important acknowledgments for last. I am grateful to my wife, Cheryl, for her steadfast support of this project and her wisdom on the topic. The publication of this book coincides with the year of our thirtieth wedding anniversary. Those decades have gone by quickly because they have been so joyful. I couldn't ask for a better life partner. Almost two decades ago, our prayers were answered with the birth of our son, Harrison. He is the apple of my eye and I could not be prouder of him. He is a kind and generous soul who brings joy to our lives every day. Together, Cheryl and Harrison make it all worthwhile.

NOTES

CHAPTER 1: JUST ASK AND MIRACLES HAPPEN

1. Jessica and her story are real, but she asked me to not use her real name.

2. In a similar vein, anxiety motivates people to seek and use advice, as Francesca Gino, Alison Wood Brooks, and Maurice E. Schweitzer document in "Anxiety, Advice, and the Ability to Discern: Feeling Anxious Motivates Individuals to Seek and Use Advice," *Journal of Personality and Social Psychology* 102, no. 3 (2012): 497–512. The researchers also learned that anxious people have trouble discerning good from bad advice, or an advisor who has a conflict of interest versus one who does not.

3. See research discussed in Adam Grant, "Givers Take All: The Hidden Dimension of Corporate Culture," *McKinsey Quarterly* (April 2013), accessed on May 22, 2018, at https://www .mckinsey.com/business-functions/organization/our -insights/givers-take-all-the-hidden-dimension-of-corporate

-culture. See also Adam Grant, *Give and Take: Why Helping Others Drives Our Success* (NY: Viking, 2013), 243.

4. Christopher G. Myers, "Is Your Company Encouraging Employees to Share What They Know?," *Harvard Business Review* (website) (November 6, 2015). In my opinion, the figures cited in this article are gross underestimates of the costs of not seeking knowledge or other resources.

5. I am indebted to Cristina's family for their generous permission to share this story.

6. Francis J. Flynn, "How Much Should I Give and How Often? The Effects of Generosity and Frequency of Favor Exchange on Social Status and Productivity," *The Academy of Management Journal* 46, no. 5 (2003): 539–53. Geller and Bamberger found that help-seeking improved individual performance if the seeker strongly endorsed an "autonomous logic" (seeking help to become competent and independent) or weakly endorsed a "dependent logic" (seeking help just to solve immediate problems). Dvora Geller and Peter A. Bamberger, "The Impact of Help Seeking on Individual Task Performance: The Moderating Effect of Help Seekers' Logics of Action," *Journal of Applied Psychology* 97, no. 2 (2012): 487–97.

7. E. W. Morrison, "Newcomer Information Seeking: Exploring Types, Modes, Sources, and Outcomes," *Academy of Management Journal,* 36, no. 3 (1993): 557–89; Tayla N. Bauer, *Onboarding New Employees: Maximizing Success* (Alexandria, VA: SHRM Foundation, 2010).

8. William P. Bridges and Wayne J. Villemez, "Informal Hiring and Income in the Labor Market," *American Sociological Review* 51 (1986): 574–82; Roberto M. Fernandez and Nancy Weinberg, "Sifting and Sorting: Personal Contacts and Hiring in a Retail Bank," *American Sociological Review* 62 (1997): 883–902; Ted Moux, "Social Capital and Finding a Job: Do Contacts Matter?," *American Sociological Review* 68 (2003): 868–98; Mark S. Granovetter, *Getting a Job,* revised edition (Chicago: University of Chicago Press, 1995); Laura K. Gee, Jason Jones, and Moira

Burke, "Social Networks and Labor Markets: How Strong Ties Relate to Job Finding on Facebook's Social Network," *Journal of Labor Economics* 35, no. 2 (April 2017): 485–518.

9. For comparisons of referrals versus job-search engines, see "Sources of Hire 2017" by SilkRoad. Accessed on April 15, 2019, at https://www.silkroad.com/.

10. S. P. Borgatti and R. Cross, "A Relational View of Information Seeking and Learning in Social Networks," *Management Science* 49, no. 4 (2003): 432–45; Susan J. Ashford, Ruth Blatt, and Don Vande Walle, "Reflections on the Looking Glass: A Review of Research on Feedback-Seeking Behavior in Organizations," *Journal of Management* 29, no. 6 (2003): 773–99. Of course, help-seeking is essential for students. See A. Ryan and P. R. Pintrich, "Achievement and Social Motivation Influences on Help Seeking in the Classroom" in S. A. Karabenick (ed.), *Strategic Help Seeking: Implications for Learning and Teaching* (Mahwah, NJ: Lawrence Erlbaum Associates, 1998), 117–39.

11. Susan J. Ashford and D. Scott DeRue, "Developing as a Leader: The Power of Mindful Engagement," *Organizational Dynamics* 41 (2012):145–54.

12. See examples in Wayne Baker, *Networking Smart* (NY: McGraw-Hill, 1994), 130–31.

13. Michael J. Arena, *Adaptive Space: How GM and Other Companies Are Positively Disrupting Themselves and Transforming into Agile Organizations* (NY: McGraw-Hill, 2018). See also, David Obstfeld, *Getting New Things Done; Networks, Brokerage, and the Assembly of Innovative Action* (Stanford, CA: Stanford University Press, 2017).

14. Jill E. Perry-Smith and Pier Vittorio Mannucci, "From Creativity to Innovation: The Social Network Drivers of the Four Phases of the Idea Journey," *Academy of Management Review* 42, no. 1 (2017): 53–79; Teresa Amabile, Colin M. Fisher, and Julianna Pillemer, "IDEO's Culture of Helping," *Harvard Business Review* (January–February 2014), accessed January 9, 2017 at https://hbr.org/2014/01/ideos-culture-of-helping;

R. S. Burt, "Structural Holes and Good Ideas," *American Journal of Sociology,* 110 (2004): 349-99; D. Obstfeld, "Social Networks, the Tertius Iungens Orientation, and Involvement in Innovation," *Administrative Science Quarterly* 50, no. 1 (2005): 100–30.

15. "Eight of Ten Americans Afflicted by Stress," *Gallup Well-Being,* December 20, 2017, accessed on April 5, 2018 at http://news .gallup.com/poll/224336/eight-americans-afflicted-stress .aspx. "U.S. Workers Least Happy with Their Work Stress and Pay," *Gallup Economy,* November 12, 2012, accessed on April 5, 2018, at http://news.gallup.com/poll/158723/workers-least -happy-work-stress-pay.aspx.

16. B. Owens, W. E. Baker, D. Sumpter, and K. Cameron, "Relational Energy at Work: Implications for Job Engagement and Job Performance," *Journal of Applied Psychology* 101, no. 1 (2016): 35–49; J. Schauebroeck and L. Fink, "Facilitating and Inhibiting Effects of Job Control and Social Support on Stress Outcomes and Role Behavior: A Contingency Model," *Journal of Organizational Behavior* 19 (1998), 167–95; Ashley V. Whillans, Elizabeth W. Dunn, Paul Smeets, Rene Bekkers, and Michael I. Norton, "Buying Time Promotes Happiness," *Proceedings of the National Academy of Sciences* (July 2017), accessed online on April 11, 2018, at http://www.pnas.org /content/early/2017/07/18/1706541114.full.

17. Peter A. Bamberger, "Employee Help-Seeking," *Research in Personnel and Human Resources Management* 28 (2009), 80; T. Amabile, C. Fisher, and J. Pillemer, "IDEO's Culture of Helping," *Harvard Business Review* 92, nos. 1 and 2 (January–February 2014), 54–61. The benefits of obtaining resources through networks are thoroughly documented in the voluminous literature on social capital. See P. S. Adler and S. Kwon, "Social Capital: Prospects for a New Concept," *Academy of Management Review* 27:17–4 (2002); Wayne Baker, *Achieving Success Through Social Capital* (San Francisco, CA: Jossey-Bass, 2000); R. Burt and D. Ronchi, "Teaching Executives to See So-

cial Capital: Results from a Field Experiment," *Social Science Research* 36, no. 3 (2007): 1156–83; R. Cross and A. Parker, *The Hidden Power of Social Networks: Understanding How Work Really Gets Done in Organizations* (Boston, MA: Harvard Business School Press, 2004); M. Kilduff and W. Tsai, *Networks and Organizations* (London: Sage Publications, 2003); R. D. Putnam, *Bowling Alone: The Collapse and Revival of American Community* (NY: Simon & Schuster, 2000); Mark C. Bolino, William H. Turnley, and James M. Bloodgood, "Citizenship Behavior and the Creation of Social Capital in Organizations," *The Academy of Management Review* 27, no. 4 (2002): 505–22.

18. Deborah Ancona and Henrik Bresman, *X-Teams* (Boston, MA: Harvard Business School Press, 2007).

19. Mark Attridge, *The Value of Employee Assistance Programs* (Norfolk, VA: EASNA, 2015), accessed on June 7, 2017, at http://www.easna.org. Eighty percent of the users of these programs are self-referrals—that is, voluntary help-seeking.

20. Li-Yun Sun, Samuel Aryee, and Kenneth S. Law, "High-Performance Human Resource Practices, Citizenship Behavior, and Organizational Performance: A Relational Perspective Source," *The Academy of Management Journal* 50, no. 3 (2007): 558–77.

21. S. J. Ashford, N. Wellman, M. Sully de Luque, K. De Stobbeleir, and M. Wollan M, "Two Roads to Effectiveness: CEO Feedback Seeking, Vision Articulation, and Firm Performance," *J Organ Behav.* 39 (2018): 82–95.

22. "Breakthrough Performance in the New Work Environment," the Corporate Executive Board Company (2012). Accessed on July 28, 2019 at eg2013ann-breakthrough-performance-in-the-new-work-environment.pdf.

23. Rich Sheridan, *Joy, Inc.* (NY: Portfolio/Penguin, 2013); S. M. Walz and B. P. Niehoff, "Organizational Citizenship Behaviors and Their Effect on Organizational Effectiveness in Limited Menu Restaurants," Best Paper Proceedings, Academy of Management conference (1996), 307–11.

CHAPTER 2: A HUMAN DILEMMA: IT'S HARD TO ASK FOR HELP

1. Garret Keizer, *Help: The Original Human Dilemma* (NY: Harper Collins, 2004).
2. F. J. Flynn and V. Lake, "If You Need Help, Just Ask: Underestimating Compliance with Direct Requests for Help," *Journal of Personality and Social Psychology* 95 (2008):128–43.
3. The exact figures are as follows (see Flynn and Lake for details): For getting strangers to complete a questionnaire, study participants predicted they would have to ask, on average, 20.5 strangers to get five completed questionnaires; they had to ask 10.5 to get five completions; for borrowing a cell phone, study participants predicted they would have to ask an average of 10.1 strangers to get three to lend their phones, in reality, they had to ask only 6.2; for getting escorted, study participants estimated that they would ask 7.2 strangers, on average, to get one escort, but they actually had to ask only 2.3.
4. Gallup's 2016 Global Civic Engagement Report, accessed on April 3, 2018, at http://news.gallup.com/reports/195581 /global-civic-engagement-report-2016.aspx?g_source=link _NEWSV9&g_medium=TOPIC&g_campaign=item_&g_content =2016%2520Global%2520Civic%2520Engagement%2520 Report.
5. Simeon Floyd, Giovanni Rossi, Julija Baranova, Joe Blythe, Mark Dingemanse, Kobin H. Kendrick, Jörg Zinken, and N. J. Enfield, "Universals and Cultural Diversity in the Expression of Gratitude," *Royal Society Open Society,* published 23 May 2018 online, accessed on September 8, 2018, at http://rsos.royalsociety publishing.org/content/5/5/180391. Data for the study comes from audiovisual recordings that were conducted unobtrusively in community and household contexts. They did not study request-response interactions in institutional or formal contexts.
6. See the Wikipedia entry on the Benjamin Franklin Effect, ac-

cessed on April 24, 2018, at https://en.wikipedia.org/wiki/Ben_Franklin_effect#cite_note-2.

7. Project Gutenberg's *Autobiography of Benjamin Franklin* by Benjamin Franklin, accessed on April 24, 2018, at https://www.gutenberg.org/files/20203/20203-h/20203-h.htm.

8. Yu Niiya, "Does a Favor Request Increase Liking Toward the Requester?," *Journal of Social Psychology* 156 (2016): 211–21.

9. F. J. Flynn, D. Newark, and V. Bohns, "Once Bitten, Twice Shy: The Effect of a Past Refusal on Future Compliance," *Social Psychological and Personality Science* 5, no. 2 (2013): 218–25.

10. See Mark Granovetter, "The Strength of Weak Ties: A Network Theory Revisited," *Sociological Theory* 1: 201–233 (1983), which reviews empirical research since his seminal paper on the topic in 1973.

11. Daniel Z. Levin, Jorge Walter, and J. Keith Murnighan, "Dormant Ties: The Value of Reconnecting," *Organization Science* 22, no. 4 (2011): 923–39. In a follow-up study, the team learned that executives feel more comfortable reconnecting with strong versus weak dormant ties, but weak dormant ties are more valuable because they provide more novelty than strong dormant ties do. See Jorge Walter, Daniel Z. Levin, and J. Keith Murnighan, "Reconnection Choices: Selecting the Most Valuable (vs. Most Preferred) Dormant Ties," *Organization Science* 26, no. 5 (2015): 1447–65.

12. I reported the results of these four national surveys in Wayne Baker, *United America: The Surprising Truth About American Values, American Identity and the 10 Beliefs That a Large Majority of Americans Hold Dear* (Canton, MI: ReadTheSpirit Books, 2014). As I write there, "It is remarkable how strongly Americans feel about these statements. Americans with a high school education (or less) are just as likely to agree with these statements as those with a college or even a graduate degree. Vast differences in income don't matter. Americans from different regions of the country are just as likely to agree with these statements. And differences in race or religion don't matter.

The wisdom of 'trust thyself' is something on which even liberals and conservatives agree."

13. A. W. Brooks, F. Gino, and M. E. Schweitzer, "Smart People Ask for (My) Advice: Seeking Advice Boosts Perceptions of Competence," *Management Science* 61, no. 6 (June 2015): 1421–35.

14. Jill E. Perry-Smith and Pier Vittorio Mannucci, "From Creativity to Innovation: The Social Network Drivers of the Four Phases of the Idea Journey," *Academy of Management Review* 42 (January 2017): 53–79.

15. For example, see research reviewed in Justin Hunt and Daniel Eisenberg, "Mental Health Problems and Help-Seeking Behavior Among College Students," *Journal of Adolescent Health* 45 (2010): 3–10.

16. Terry Gaspard, "How Being Too Self-Reliant Can Destroy Your Relationship," *Huffington Post,* January 3, 2015, accessed on January 7, 2017, at http://www.huffingtonpost.com/terry -gaspard-msw-licsw/how-self-reliance-can-destroy-a -relationship_b_6071906.html.

17. Fiona Lee, "The Social Costs of Seeking Help," *Journal of Applied Behavioral Science* 38, no. 1 (March 2002):17–35. See also G. S. Van der Vegt, J. S. Bunderson, and A. Oosterhof, "Expertness Diversity and Interpersonal Helping in Teams," *Academy of Management Journal* 49, no. 5 (2006): 877–93.

18. Brooks, Gino, and Schweitzer, "Smart People Ask for (My) Advice."

19. Ashleigh Shelby Rosette and Jennifer Mueller, "Are Male Leaders Penalized for Seeking Help? The Influence of Gender and Asking Behaviors on Competence Perceptions," *The Leadership Quarterly* 26 (2015): 749–62.

20. D. Miller, L. Karakowsky, "Gender Influences as an Impediment to Knowledge Sharing: When Men and Women Fail to Seek Peer Feedback," *J. Psychol.* 139, no. 2 (2005):101–18.

21. S. E. Taylor, D. K. Sherman, H. S. Kim, J. Jarcho, K. Takagi, and M. S. Dunagan, "Culture and Social Support: Who Seeks

It and Why?," *Journal of Personality and Social Psychology* 87 (2004): 354. S. E. Taylor, W. T. Welch, H. S. Kim, and D. K. Sherman, "Cultural Differences in the Impact of Social Support on Psychological and Biological Stress Responses." *Psychological Science* 18 (2007): 831–37. H. S. Kim, D. K. Sherman, and S. E. Taylor, "Culture and Social Support," *American Psychologist* 63 (2008): 518. For a summary of cultural differences in feedback seeking, see Susann J. Ashford, Katleeen De Stobberleir, and Mrudula Nujella, "To Seek or Not to Seek: Recent Developments in Feedback-Seeing Literature." *Annual Review of Organizational Psychology and Organizational Behavior* 3 (2016): 213–39, see esp. p. 225.

22. Ibid.

23. Bamberger, "Employee Help-Seeking"; Dvora Geller and Peter A. Bamberger, "The Impact of Help Seeking on Individual Task Performance: The Moderating Effect of Help Seekers' Logics of Action," *Journal of Applied Psychology* 97, no. 2 (2012): 487–97.

24. Arie Nadler, "Relationships, Esteem and Achievement Perspectives on Autonomous and Dependent Help Seeking," in Stuart A. Karabenick (ed.). *Strategic Help Seeking: Implications for Knowledge Acquisition* (New Jersey: Erlbaum Publishing Co., 1998), 51–93; Bamberger, "Employee Help-Seeking."

25. Nadler, "Relationships, Esteem and Achievement Perspectives on Autonomous and Dependent Help Seeking," 63–64.

26. Nadler, "Relationships, Esteem and Achievement Perspectives on Autonomous and Dependent Help Seeking," 64.

27. Amy Edmondson, "Psychological Safety and Learning Behavior in Work Teams," *Administrative Science Quarterly* 44, no. 2 (1999): 350–83. See also Amy Edmondson, *Teaming: How Organizations Learn, Innovate, and Compete in the Knowledge Economy* (San Francisco, CA: Jossey-Bass, 2012); Amy Edmondson, *The Fearless Organization: Creating Psychological Safety in the Workplace for Learning, Innovation, and Growth* (Hoboken, NJ: John Wiley & Sons, 2019).

28. Help seekers are reluctant to ask experts for help if they per-

ceive the experts to be untrustworthy. See, for example, David A. Hofmann, Zhike Lei, and Adam M. Grant, "Seeking Help in the Shadow of Doubt: The Sensemaking Processes Underlying How Nurses Decide Whom to Ask for Advice," *Journal of Applied Psychology* 94, no. 5 (2009): 1261–70.

29. Amy C. Edmondson, "The Competitive Imperative of Learning," *Harvard Business Review* (July–August, 2008).

30. Julia Rozovsky, "The Five Keys to a Successful Google Team," The Watercooler Blog, November 17, 2015, accessed on January 13, 2017, at https://rework.withgoogle.com/blog/five-keys -to-a-successful-google-team/.

31. Email exchange with Kathryn Dekas, November 20, 2018. See also Kathryn H. Dekas, Talya N. Bauer, Brian Welle, Jennifer Kurkoski, and Stacy Sullivan, "Organizational Citizenship Behavior, Version 2.0: A Review and Qualitative Investigation of OCBs for Knowledge Workers at Google and Beyond," *The Academy of Management Perspective* 27 (2013): 219–37.

32. Richard Sheridan, *Joy, Inc.: How We Built a Workplace People Love* (NY: Portfolio/Penguin (2013): 94.

33. Cassandra Chambers and Wayne E. Baker, "Robust Systems of Cooperation in the Presence of Rankings," *Organization Science* (in press).

34. I first used this example in Wayne Baker, "5 Ways to Get Better at Asking for Help," *Harvard Business Review,* December 18, 2014 [digital article], accessed on January 4, 2017, at https://hbr.org/2014/12/5-ways-to-get-better-at-asking-for -help.

35. Wayne E. Baker and Nathaniel Bulkley, "Paying It Forward vs. Rewarding Reputation: Mechanisms of Generalized Reciprocity," *Organization Science* 25, no. 5 (2014): 1493–1510.

36. Adam Grant, *Give and Take* (NY: Viking, 2013), 5.

37. This principle has a long pedigree. As Victorian philosopher and psychologist William James put it, "If you want quality, act as if you already have it." Richard Wiseman makes this principle the core of his book *The As If Principle* (NY: Simon &

Schuster, 2012). Shook's pyramid model (in my Chapter 2) is quite similar to Edgar H. Schein's culture change model, as Shook acknowledges. See, for example, Shein's *Organizational Culture and Leadership,* 4th edition (San Francisco, CA: John Wiley & Sons, 2010).

38. John Shook, "How to Change a Culture," *MIT Sloan Management Review* 51 (2010): 66. Reproduced with permission. Copyright © 2010 from MIT Sloan Management Review/ Massachusetts Institute of Technology. All rights reserved. Distributed by Tribune Content Agency, LLC.

CHAPTER 3: THE LAW OF GIVING *AND* RECEIVING

1. Andrew Jacobs, "Celebrity Chefs Turn Wasted Olympic Food into Meals for Homeless," *New York Times* (August 14, 2016). To learn more, visit the nonprofit's website, http://www.refettorio gastromotiva.org/english/.

2. To read more about Bottura, see: Francesca Gino, *Rebel Talent: Why It Pays to Break the Rules at Work and in Life* (NY: Dey St., an imprint of William Morrow, 2018).

3. "Living the Generous Life: Reflections on Giving and Receiving," edited by Wayne Muller and Megan Scribner. A Project of The Fetzer Institute (n.d.), accessed on March 4, 2017, at http://fetzer.org/resources/living-generous-life.

4. Julie Ray, "Billions Worldwide Help Others in Need," Gallup (September 20, 2016). Gallup conducted its survey in 2015 in 140 countries, accessed March 5, 2017, at http://www.gallup .com/poll/195659/billions-worldwide-help-others-need.aspx? utm_source=alert&utm_medium=email&utm_content=more link&utm_campaign=syndication.

5. Jenifer J. Partch and Richard T. Kinnier, "Values and Messages Conveyed in College Commencement Speeches," *Current Psychology* 30, no. 1 (2011): 81–92.

6. "Living the Generous Life," 8.

7. Adam Grant, *Give and Take* (NY: Viking, 2013), 158. Similarly,

Deepak Chopra considers the Law of Giving and Receiving to be one of the seven spiritual laws of success.

8. Grant, *Give and Take,* 5.

9. Wayne Baker, *Achieving Success Through Social Capital* (San Francisco, CA: Jossey-Bass, 2000), 139.

10. Adam M. Grant and Reb Rebele, "Generosity Burnout," *Harvard Business Review* (February 1, 2017) [digital article], accessed on March 4, 2017, at https://hbr.org/generosity.

11. James Andreoni, "Impure Altruism and Donations to Public Goods: A Theory of Warm-Glow Giving," *Economic Journal* 100, no. 401 (1990): 464–77. The warm glow of giving may be hardwired. For example, it has been documented in children under the age of two. See Lara B. Aknin, J. Kiley Hamlin, and Elizabeth W. Dunn, "Giving Leads to Happiness in Young Children," *PLOS One,* June 14, 2012, accessed on March 9, 2017, at http://journals.plos.org/plosone/article?id=10.1371/journal.pone.0039211.

12. Francis J. Flynn, "How Much Should I Give and How Often? The Effects of Generosity and Frequency of Favor Exchange on Social Status and Productivity," *The Academy of Management Journal* 46, no. 5 (2003): 539–53. See also "The Gift Relationship," *Economist* [London, England] April 10, 2004: 59. *The Economist Historical Archive, 1843–2013,* accessed on March 1, 2017, at http://www.economist.com/node/2582734.

13. Christian Smith and Hillary Davidson, *The Paradox of Generosity* (NY: Oxford University Press, 2014), 94.

14. Christina S. Melvin, "Professional Compassion Fatigue: What Is the True Cost of Nurses Caring for the Dying?," *International Journal of Palliative Nursing* 18, no. 12 (2012): 606–11. See also Sherry E. Showalter, "Compassion Fatigue: What Is It? Why Does It Matter? Recognizing the Symptoms, Acknowledging the Impact, Developing the Tools to Prevent Compassion Fatigue, and Strengthen the Professional Already Suffering from the Effects," *American Journal of Hospice and Palliative Medicine* 27, no. 4 (2010): 239–42; Laura McCray, Peter F. Cronholm, Hillary R. Bogner, Joseph J. Gallo, and Richard A.

Neill, "Resident Physician Burnout: Is There Hope?," *Family Medicine* 40, no. 9 (2008): 626–32; Nadine Najjar, Louranne W. Davis, Kathleen Beck-Coon, and Caroline Carney Doebbeling, "Compassion Fatigue: A Review of the Research to Date and Relevance to Cancer-Care Providers," *Journal of Health Psychology* 14, no. 2 (2009): 267–77.

15. Wayne E. Baker and Nathaniel Bulkley, "Paying It Forward vs. Rewarding Reputation: Mechanisms of Generalized Reciprocity," *Organization Science* 25, no. 5 (2014):1493–1510.

16. Wayne E. Baker and Sheen S. Levine, "Mechanisms of Generalized Exchange," October 1, 2013. Available at SSRN: https://ssrn.com/abstract=1352101 or http://dx.doi.org/10.2139/ssrn.1352101.

17. Grant, *Give and Take,* 244.

18. Flynn, "How Much Should I Give and How Often?"

19. Research has firmly established the relationship of social capital and performance for individuals, teams, organizations, and even nations (see endnotes to Chapter 1 for references).

20. A longitudinal study of health practices and outcomes among residents of Alameda County is one of the most famous. For an early analysis that established the link between social isolation and risk of death, see L. F. Berkman and S. L. Syme, "Social Networks, Host Resistance, and Mortality: A Nine-Year Follow-Up Study of Alameda County Residents," *American Journal of Epidemiology* 109, no. 2 (1979): 186–204. A summary of findings is available in Jeff Housman and Steve Dorman, "The Alameda County Study: A Systematic, Chronological Review," *American Journal of Health Education* 26, no. 5 (2005): 302–8. A meta-analytic review of 148 studies further establishes the link between social networks and mortality risk. Julianne Holt-Lunstad, Timothy B. Smith, and J. Bradley Layton, "Social Relationshps and Mortality Risk: A Meta-Analytic Review," *PLOS Medicine* (July 27, 2010), accessed on March 12, 2017, at http://journals.plos.org/plosmedicine/article?id=10.1371/journal.pmed.1000316.

21. Carla M. Perissinotto, Irena Stijacic Cenzer, and Kenneth E. Covinsky, "Loneliness in Older Persons: A Predictor of Functional Decline and Death," *JAMA Internal Medicine* 172, no. 14 (2012):1078–84.

22. John T. Cacioppo and Stephanie Cacioppo, "Social Relationships and Health: The Toxic Effects of Perceived Social Isolation," *Social and Personality Psychology Compass* 8, no. 2 (2014): 58.

23. Flynn, "How Much Should I Give and How Often?"

24. Teresa Amabile, Colin M. Fisher, and Julianna Pillemer, "IDEO's Culture of Helping," *Harvard Business Review,* January–February 2014, accessed January 9, 2017, at https://hbr.org /2014/01/ideos-culture-of-helping.

CHAPTER 4: GET STARTED NOW: FIGURING OUT WHAT YOU NEED AND ASKING FOR IT

1. Sources: Interview on March 15, 2019, and "Miss Kim's Kicks Off in Kerrytown," Zingerman's Newsletter, Issue 257, Jan–Feb 2017: 3–4. Some material is edited for clarity and shortened for brevity. Some material is based on personal interviews and emails with Ji Hye.

2. This story is real, but I omit identifying details to preserve anonymity.

3. For example, Sonja Lyubomirsky, *The How of Happiness: A New Approach to Getting the Life You Want* (NY: Penguin, 2007).

4. Lyubomirsky, *The How of Happiness,* 205–26.

5. Ibid.

6. This story is real, but I changed the name to preserve anonymity.

7. Email exchange, March 9–10, 2019.

8. Several of these examples come from Wayne E. Baker and Nathaniel Bulkley, "Paying It Forward vs. Rewarding Reputation: Mechanisms of Generalized Reciprocity," *Organization Science* 25, no. 5 (2014): 1493–1510.

9. Lawrence L. Lippitt, *Preferred Futuring: Envision the Future You Want and Unleash the Energy to Get There* (San Francisco, CA: Berrett-Koehler, 1998).

10. See, for example, Ari Weinzweig, *The Power of Beliefs in Business, Zingerman's Guide to Good Leading, Part 4* (Ann Arbor, MI: Zingerman's Press, 2016), 416.

11. G. T. Doran, "There's a S.M.A.R.T. Way to Write Management's Goals and Objectives," *Management Review,* AMA Forum 70, no. 11: 35–36.

12. Simon Sinek, *Start With Why: How Great Leaders Inspire Everyone to Take Action* (NY: Portfolio/Penguin, 2009).

13. Rob Cross, Andrew Parker, Laurence Prusak, and Stephen P. Borgatti, "Knowing What We Know: Supporting Knowledge Creation and Sharing in Social Networks," *Organizational Dynamics* 30, no. 2 (2001):100–20.

14. For an example in the banking context, see Mark S. Mizruchi and Linda B. Stearns, "Getting Deals Done: The Use of Social Networks in Bank Decision-Making," *American Sociological Review* 66, no. 5 (2001): 647–71.

15. Sheen S. Levine and Michael J. Prietula, "How Knowledge Transfer Impacts Performance: A Multi-Level Model of Benefits and Liabilities," *Organization Science,* 23, no. 6 (2012), 1748–66. Sheen S. Levine, "The Strength of Performative Ties: Three Essays on Knowledge, Social Networks, and Exchange," January 1, 2005. *Dissertations available from ProQuest,* http://repository.upenn.edu/dissertations/AAI3197702.

16. Levine, "The Strength of Performative Ties."

17. Levine and Prietula, "How Knowledge Transfer Impacts Performance," and Levine, "The Strength of Performative Ties."

18. Daniel Z. Levin, Jorge Walter, and J. Keith Murnighan, "Dormant Ties: The Value of Reconnecting," *Organization Science* 22, no. 4 (2011): 923–39. See Jorge Walter, Daniel Z. Levin, and J. Keith Murnighan, "Reconnection Choices: Selecting the Most Valuable (vs. Most Preferred) Dormant Ties," *Organization Science* 26, no. 5 (2015): 1447–65.

19. Personal communication with Jeff DeGraff, May 19, 2017. To learn more about the Innovatrium, visit http://www .innovatrium.org.

20. Personal communication with Jeff DeGraff, April 17, 2018.

21. Vanessa K. Bohns, "A Face-to-Face Request Is 34 Times More Successful than an Email," *Harvard Business Review* [digital version], April 11, 2017, accessed on May 15, 2017, at https:// hbr.org/2017/04/a-face-to-face-request-is-34-times-more -successful-than-an-email. Based on research by M. Mahdi Roghanizad and Vanessa K. Bohns, "Ask in Person: You're Less Persuasive Than You Think Over Email," *Journal of Experimental Psychology* 69 (March 2017): 223–26. Note, however, that this study is based on making requests to strangers, not people you know or knew in the past. Nonetheless, it underscores a tendency to overestimate the effectiveness of email as the way to make requests.

22. Jia Jiang, *Rejection Proof: How I Beat Fear and Became Invincible* (NY: Harmony, 2015).

23. Jia summarizes these lessons at the end of chapters, in Chapter 11, and in the appendix to his book.

24. Jiang, *Rejection Proof,* 94–95.

25. Jia discusses the rejection rates for several blockbuster books, including *Harry Potter and the Philosopher's Stone,* 89–90.

CHAPTER 5: TOOLS FOR TEAMS

1. Deborah Ancona and Henrik Bresman, *X-Teams: How to Build Teams that Lead, Innovate, and Succeed* (Boston, MA: Harvard Business School Press, 2007). See, especially, pages 160–77.

2. Ancona and Bresman, *X-Teams,* 167.

3. Amy C. Edmondson, *Teaming* (San Francisco, CA; Jossey-Bass, 2012); Ancona and Bresman, *X-Teams.*

4. Ashford and DeRue, "Developing as a Leader," and Scott D. DeRue and Susan J. Asford, "Who Will Lead and Who Will Follow? A Social Process of Leadership Identity Construction in

Organizations," *Academy of Management Review* 35 (2010): 627–47.

5. Ancona and Bresman, *X-Teams,* 168.

6. See Southwest Airlines fact sheet at https://www.swamedia .com/pages/corporate-fact-sheet.

7. For example, in 2016, the airline received 342,664 résumés and hired 7,207 new employees, according to Southwest's website (ibid).

8. Julie Weber, "How Southwest Airlines Hires Such Dedicated People," *Harvard Business Review* [digital version], accessed on January 9, 2018, https://hbr.org/2015/12/how-southwest -airlines-hires-such-dedicated-people.

9. Weber, "How Southwest Airlines Hires Such Dedicated People."

10. Ingrid M. Nembhard and Amy C. Edmondson, "Making It Safe: The Effects of Leader Inclusiveness and Professional Status on Psychological Safety and Improvement Efforts in Health Care Teams," *Journal of Organizational Behavior,* 27 (2006): 941–66.

11. Ibid.

12. Amy Edmondson, "Psychological Safety and Learning Behavior in Work Teams," *Administrative Science Quarterly* 44:350–83 (1999).

13. This is a true story. To protect the protagonist, I changed the person's name and made identifying details in the story anonymous.

14. Julia Rozovsky, "The Five Keys to a Successful Google Team," The Watercooler Blog, November 17, 2015, accessed on January 13, 2017, at https://rework.withgoogle.com/blog/five-keys -to-a-successful-google-team/.

15. Gary Klein, "Performing a Project Premortem," *Harvard Business Review*, September 2007, accessed on December 3, 2018, at https://hbr.org/2007/09/performing-a-project-premortem.

16. Teresa Amabile, Collin M. Fisher, and Julianna Pillemer, "IDEO's Culture of Helping," *Harvard Business Review,* January–February issue (2014). This section is based on interviews and email exchanges I had with Heather Currier Hunt.

17. Personal communication, May 9, 2017.

18. Personal communication, October 31, 2018.

19. Edmondson, "The Competitive Imperative of Learning."

20. Personal communication, December 6, 2018, and subsequent email exchanges.

21. Quoted in John Eades, "7 Leadership Lessons from the CEO of a Multibillion-Dollar Company," *Inc.* (April 3, 2017), accessed on March 25, 2019, at https://www.inc.com/john-eades /7-leadership-lessons-from-the-ceo-of-a-multi-billion-dollar -company.html.

22. Email exchanges with Christina Keller and Fred Keller, March 25, 2019.

23. Joel Podolny, "Interview with John Clendenin" [video]. (Stanford, CA: Stanford Business School, 1992).

24. Ryan W. Quinn and J. Stuart Bunderson, "Could We Huddle on This Project? Participant Learning in Newsroom Conversations," *Journal of Management* 42 (2016): 386–418.

25. Amabile, Fisher, and Pillemer, "IDEO's Culture of Helping."

26. Dan Radigan, "Stand-ups for Agile Teams" (n.d.), accessed on April 23, 2018, at https://www.atlassian.com/agile/scrum /standups.

27. Personal communication, April 24, 2018.

28. Michael A. Orzen and Thomas A. Paider, *The Lean IT Field Guide: A Roadmap for Your Transformation* (Boca Raton, FL: CRC Press/Taylor & Francis Group, 2016), 48.

29. Adam Grant, *Give and Take* (NY: Viking, 2013), 241.

30. Ashley E. Hardin, "Getting Acquainted: How Knowing About Colleague's Personal Lives Impacts Workplace Interactions, for Better and Worse," doctoral dissertation, University of Michigan Ross School of Business (2017).

31. "Hack Your Happiness: How Doing Favors for Others Can Make You Happier," *Good Morning America,* December 26, 2018, accessed on March 26, 2019, at https://www.good morningamerica.com/wellness/video/hack-happiness-favors -make-happier-60016878.

32. Henri Lipmanowicz and Keith McCandless, *The Surprising Power of Liberating Structures: Simple Rules to Unleash a Culture of Innovation* (Seattle, Washington: Liberating Structures Press, 2013). In this book, the authors outline thirty-three proven practices that enable groups of people to interact and work together in new and productive ways. These "liberating structures" have been implemented in organizations far and wide, everywhere from healthcare to academia to the military to consulting firms to global business enterprises. The URL for the Liberating Structures website is www.liberatingstructures .com. You can get the Liberating Structures app at the app store.

33. Source: DoSomething.org website, accessed on January 31, 2018, at https://www.dosomething.org/us/about/who-we -are.

34. DoSomething.org was a finalist in the Positive Business Practice competition at the University of Michigan Ross School of Business. This practice is described in their video submission, available at: http://positivebusinessproject.com/past-winners/.

35. Personal communication with Ron May, December 20, 2018, and March 25, 2019. Ron is now retired and donates his time and wisdom as an executive in residence at the Center for Positive Organizations. For more information on the kata approach Ron used, see Mike Rother, *Toyota Kata: Managing People for Improvement, Adaptiveness, and Superior Results* (NY: McGraw-Hill, 2010).

36. Personal communication with Kevin Blue, June 13, 2017.

37. Nembhard and Edmondson, "Making it Safe."

CHAPTER 6: ASKING ACROSS BOUNDARIES

1. I am grateful to Dave Scholten for responding to my request for help when I was searching for new examples for this book. He provided the details about the mini-game. I am grateful to Kent Power for permission to tell their story.

2. Dave Scholten has played this mini-game at other clients as well. All have experienced positive results.

3. Gardner, *Smart Collaboration: How Professionals and Their Firms Succeed by Breaking Down Silos* (Boston, MA: Harvard Business Review Press, 2017) 20–41. See also Sheen S. Levine and Michael J. Prietula, "How Knowledge Transfer Impacts Performance," *Organization Science*, 23, no. 6 (2012), 1748–66, and Sheen S. Levine, "The Strength of Performative Ties: Three Essays on Knowledge, Social Networks, and Exchange" (January 1, 2005). Dissertations available from ProQuest. Paper AAI3197702. http://repository.upenn.edu/dissertations/AAI3197702.

4. Email exchange, January 7–9, 2019.

5. Deborah Ancona and Henrick Bresman, *X-Teams: How to Build Teams That Lead, Innovate, and Succeed* (Boston, MA: Harvard Business School Press, 2007), 218–19.

6. Scott E. Page, *The Diversity Bonus* (Princeton, NJ: Princeton University Press, 2017).

7. Page, *The Diversity Bonus*, 2.

8. Co-location also facilitated collaboration. GM's new Powertrain Performance and Racing Center co-locates engineers from the production powertrain operations and engineers from GM's racing program. Co-location and physical proximity facilitate the ongoing exchange of ideas, knowledge, information, and advice. See James M. Amend, "New GM Powertrain Facility to Speed Engine Tech Transfer," *WardsAuto* (Feb 2, 2016), accessed on February 9, 2018, at http://wardsauto.com/engines/new-gm-powertrain-facility-speed-engine-tech-transfer.

9. Email exchange, March 29, 2019.

10. Described in Michael J. Arena, *Adaptive Space: How GM and Other Companies Are Positively Disrupting Themselves and Transforming into Agile Organizations* (NY: McGraw-Hill, 2018).

11. Arena, *Adaptive Space*, 125–26.

12. This is a real example, but for purposes of confidentiality, I changed the person's name and removed other identifying information.

13. Emily Moore, "7 Companies with Amazing Office Rotation Options," *Glassdoor,* November 28, 2017, accessed at https://www.glassdoor.com/blog/companies-with-office-rotation-options/.

14. Jaime Ortega, "Job Rotation as a Learning Mechanism," *Management Science* 47, no. 10 (2001): 1361–70.

15. Interview on January 11, 2018, and email exchange on February 25, 2019.

16. Email exchange, February 13, 2019.

17. Phone interview, February 5, 2019.

18. https://www.ypo.org/about-ypo/, accessed on February 6, 2019.

19. Email exchange, February 7, 2019.

20. Innovate Brew website and video, accessed on February 12, 2018, at http://innovateblue.umich.edu/research/innovate-brew/.

21. Ibid.

22. Interview, January 28, 2019.

23. Interview, February 11, 2019, and email exchange, April 29, 2019.

24. As of January 2019, per "Statista: The Statistics Portal," accessed at https://www.statista.com/statistics/258749/most-popular-global-mobile-messenger-apps/.

25. Interview, January 28, 2019.

26. Email exchange, February 15, 2019.

27. Veronica Gilrane, "Working Together When We're Not Together." Working at Google blog, April 4, 2019. Accessed on June 9, 2019 at https://blog.google/inside-google/working-google/working-together-when-were-not-together/.

28. Paul Leonardi and Tsedal Neeley, "What Managers Need to Know About Social Tools," *Harvard Business Review,* November–December issue (2017).

29. P. M. Leonardi, "Ambient Awareness and Knowledge Acquisition: Using Social Media to Learn 'Who Knows What' and 'Who Knows Whom,'" *MIS Quarterly* 39 (2015): 747–76.

30. I thank my colleague Jose Uribe for providing me with this network diagram.

31. Gardner, *Smart Collaboration*, 175–83.

32. Gardner, *Smart Collaboration*, 181–82.

33. Dan Ranta, "The Power of Connections at ConocoPhillips," *Slideshare*, accessed on February 14, 2018, at https://www.slideshare.net/SIKM/dan-ranta-power-of-connections-at-conocophillips. See also P. Gray and D. Ranta, "Networks of Excellence," in R. Cross, R. J. Thomas, J. Singer, S. Colella, and Y. Silverstone (eds), *The Organizational Network Fieldbook* (San Francisco, CA: Jossey-Bass, 2010).

34. Skype interview, February 28, 2018.

35. Charles Steinfield, Joan M. DiMicco, Nicole B. Ellison, and Cliff Lampe, "Bowling Online: Social Networking and Social Capital with the Organization," proceedings of the fourth international conference on Communities and Technologies (2009), 246.

36. Joan DiMicco, David R. Millen, Werner Geyer, Casey Dugan, Beth Brownholtz, and Michael Muller, "Motivations for Social Networking at Work," conference paper, *ACM* (2008), 716.

37. Jennifer Thom, David Millen, and Joan DiMicco, "Removing Gamification from an Enterprise SNS," *Proceedings of the ACM 2012 Conference on Computer Supported Cooperative Work* (NY: ACM, 2012).

38. Analysis in Thom, Millen, and DiMicco, "Removing Gamification."

39. Cliff Lampe, Rick Wash, Alcides Velasquez, and Elif Ozkaya, "Motivations to Participate in Online Communities," proceedings of the SIGCHI conference of human factors in competing system, *ACM* (2010), 1927–36.

40. Jacob C. Fisher, Jonathon Cummings, and Yong-Mi Kim, "Abandoning Innovations: Network Evidence on Enterprise Collaboration Software," unpublished manuscript (University of Michigan Institute for Social Research).

41. Gardner, *Smart Collaboration*, 175.

CHAPTER 7: RECOGNITION AND REWARDS

1. "Gallup's 2017 State of the American Workplace," accessed at https://www.gallup.com/workplace/238085/state-american -workplace-report-2017.aspx; see also "The ROI of Recognition in Building a More Human Workplace," Globoforce Workplace Research Institute, 2016 Survey Report accessed at http://go .globoforce.com/rs/862-JIQ-698/images/ROIofRecognition .pdf and L. Anik, L. B. Aknin, M. I. Norton, E. W. Dunn, and J. Quoidbach, "Prosocial Bonuses Increase Employee Satisfaction and Team Performance," *PLOS ONE* 8, no. 9 (2013): e75509. doi:10.1371/journal.pone.0075509.

2. Ibid.

3. "The ROI of Recognition in Building a More Human Workplace," Globoforce.

4. This story comes from a Gallup article by Jennifer Robison, "In Praise of Praising Your Employees," Gallup website, November 90, 2006, accessed at https://www.gallup.com/workplace /236951/praise-praising-employees.aspx?version=print. My discussion of this story contains paraphrased and quoted material from this article. I updated the facts about Granite's revenue and David Grazian's job title.

5. I also interviewed Dave Grazian on May 13, 2019. Now retired, he founded and is president of Youth NOW.

6. Tómas Bjarnason, "Social Recognition and Employees' Organizational Support," *Göteborg Studies in Sociology* No. 27 (2009). Department of Sociology, Göteborg University.

7. Interview, January 13, 2019. In addition, see David Sturt, Todd Nordstrom, Kevin Ames, and Gary Beckstrand, *Appreciate: Celebrating People, Inspiring Greatness* (Salt Lake City, UT: O.C. Tanner Institute Publishing).

8. "Having a Calling and Crafting a Job: The Case of Candice Billups." Center for Positive Organizations, University of Michigan Ross School of Business. https://positiveorgs.bus.umich .edu/teaching-resources/teaching-cases/.

9. Christopher P. Cerasoli, Jessica M. Nicklin, and Michael T. Ford, "Intrinsic Motivation and Extrinsic Incentives Jointly Predict Performance: A 40-Year Meta-Analysis," *Psychological Bulletin,* 140 (2014): 980–1008.

10. James M. Kouzes and Barry Z. Posner, *Encouraging the Heart* (San Francisco, CA: John Wiley & Sons, Inc., 2003).

11. Ari Weinzweig, *A Lapsed Anarchists Approach to Building a Great Business: Zingerman's Guide to Good Leading Part 1* (Ann Arbor, MI: Zingerman's Press, 2010), 213.

12. Marian J. Their, *Coaching Clues* (London: Nicholas Brealey Publishing, 2003).

13. Dani Fankhauser, "The ROI of Recognition in the Workplace," Give and Take, Inc. blog post (October 4, 2018), accessed at https://giveandtakeinc.com/blog/culture/the-roi-of-recognition -in-the-workplace/.

14. This example was provided to me via email by Betsy Erwin, senior associate director and education lead, Center for Positive Organizations at the University of Michigan Ross School of Business, February 26, 2019.

15. Robert A. Emmons and Michael E. McCullough, "Counting Blessings Versus Burdens: An Experimental Investigation of Gratitude and Subjective Well-Being in Daily Life," *Journal of Personality and Social Psychology* 84, no. 2 (February 2003), 377–89. See also research findings from the O.C. Tanner Institute discussed in David Sturt, Todd Nordstrom, Kevin Ames, and Gary Beckstrand, *Appreciate* and Adam M. Grant and Francesca Gino, "A Little Thanks Goes a Long Way: Explaining Why Gratitude Expressions Motivate Prosocial Behavior," *Journal of Personality and Social Psychology* 98, no. 6 (June 2010), 946–55.

16. Laszlo Bock, *Work Rules!* (London: John Murray, 2015), 249–50.

17. Bock, *Work Rules!* 250–51.

18. Bock, *Work Rules!* 251.

19. Interview on December 11, 2018; email exchange on January 10–12, 2019.

20. "Using Recognition and Other Workplace Efforts to Engage Employees," Society for Human Resource Management and Globoforce (2018), accessed online at https://www.shrm.org /hr-today/trends-and-forecasting/research-and-surveys /Documents/SHRM-GloboforceEmployeeRecognition%202018 .pdf.

21. "The ROI of Recognition in Building a More Human Work-place," Globoforce.

22. Interview, January 21, 2019.

23. Personal communication, 2017. GTB won the 2015 Positive Business Project Award for this practice. You can learn more about it at https://www.youtube.com/watch?v=j9GmcAAqRAU.

24. This is a true story, but the protagonist asked me to not provide identifying information.

25. Steven Kerr, "On the Folly of Rewarding A, While Hoping for B," *The Academy of Management Executive* 9, no. 1 (1995), 7–14.

26. Phone interview, January 28, 2019.

27. Marcus Buckingham and Ashley Goodall, "Reinventing Performance Management," *Harvard Business Review* (April 2015).

28. Peter Cappelli and Anna Tavis, "The Performance Management Revolution," *Harvard Business Review* (October 2015).

29. Phone interview, April 5, 2018.

30. The four questions are: "This person is ready for promotion today." "The person is at risk of low performance." "I would always want this person on my team." "I would give this person the highest possible compensation." For details, see Buckingham and Goodall, "Reinventing Performance Management."

31. Source: https://www.greatgame.com/blog/employee-engagement /8-awesome-minigame-ideas-generated-practitioners, accessed February 6, 2018.

32. The bottom-line boost can be astronomical, such as the financial impact of mini-games played at a transportation parts manufacturer with annual revenues of $60 million. They played thirty-eight mini-games at the same time; the direct benefit was an increase of $450,000 in net profit. They esti-

mate that, to date, all the games they have played have improved net profit by $1.7 million.

33. Jack Stack with Bo Burlingham, *The Great Game of Business, Expanded and Updated: The Only Sensible Way to Run a Company* (NY: Crown Business, 2013). The original edition was published in 1992. The Great Game methodology is also called "Open Book Management." John Case coined the term "open-book management." See his *Open-book Management: The Coming Business Revolution* (NY: HarperCollins, 1995).

34. This summary of SRC's gainsharing plan is based on chapter 7 in Stack with Burlingham, *The Great Game of Business*, 157–83.

35. Stack with Burlingham, *The Great Game of Business*, 162.

36. Stack with Burlingham, *The Great Game of Business*, 159.

INDEX

ABOUT THE AUTHOR

WAYNE BAKER is Robert P. Thome Professor of Business Administration and professor of management and organizations at the University of Michigan Ross School of Business. He is faculty director of the Center for Positive Organizations, and Faculty Co-Director of Leading with Impact, a partnership between General Motors and Executive Education.

His research, teaching, speaking, and consulting focus on social capital, social networks, generosity, positive organizational scholarship, and values. He has published numerous scholarly articles and six books. His leadership and management articles appear in *Harvard Business Review, Chief Executive* magazine, *MIT Sloan Management Review,* and elsewhere.

He is a co-founder, strategic advisor, and board member of Give and Take, Inc., developers of the Givitas collaborative technology platform based on the principles in *All You Have to Do Is Ask.*

Prior to joining the University of Michigan faculty, he was on the faculty at the University of Chicago business school. He earned his PhD in sociology from Northwestern University and was a post-doctoral research fellow at Harvard University. He resides with his wife, son, and a Birman cat in Ann Arbor, Michigan.

To learn more, visit: waynebaker.org.

ABOUT THE TYPE

This book was set in Bookman, which was the name given to the original typeface Old Style Antique by Wadsworth A. Parker (1864–1938) at the turn of the last century. The first cutting of Old Style Antique was made in 1858 by Miller & Richard, a Scottish foundry, as a result of the need for a typeface with greater weight than the standard old-style faces possessed.